# 4/20
## A Mother's Fight to Survive

## ALICE NEHME

DocUmeant *Publishing*
244 5th Avenue
Suite G-200
NY, NY 10001
646-233-4366
www.DocUmeantPublishing.com

© 2024 All rights reserved. Alice Nehme

**Published by**
DocUmeant Publishing
244 5th Avenue, Suite G-200
NY, NY 10001

646–233–4366

**Limit of Liability and Disclaimer of Warranty**: The publisher has used its best efforts in preparing this book and the information provided herein is provided "as is".

The author has attempted to recreate events, locales, and conversations from their memories of them. In order to maintain their anonymity, in some instances, the names of individuals and places may have changed, as well as some identifying characteristics and details such as physical properties, occupations, and places of residence.

No part of this book may be reproduced or transmitted in any form or by any means, electronic or mechanical, including photocopying, recording or by any information storage or retrieval system, except as may be expressly permitted by law or in writing from the publisher, or except by a reviewer who may quote brief passages in review to be printed in a magazine, newspaper, or online website.

Permission should be addressed in writing to:
publisher@DocUmeantPublishing.com

Edited by Philip S. Marks

Cover Design, Illustrations, and layout by DocUmeant Designs
www.DocUmeantDesigns.com

Library of Congress Control Number: 2024940680

ISBN: 9781957832432 (pbk)

ISBN: 9781957832449 (ePub)

To all the women in the world who believed life would be amazing but had their independence and self-worth snatched away, this book is for you.

> "Develop enough courage so that you can stand up for yourself and then stand up for someone else."
>
> MAYA ANGELOU

# Contents

Acknowledgment . . . . . . . . . . . . . . . . . . . . . . . . . . . ix
The Story . . . . . . . . . . . . . . . . . . . . . . . . . . . . . . . . 1
The Beginning . . . . . . . . . . . . . . . . . . . . . . . . . . . . . 4
Married Life Begins . . . . . . . . . . . . . . . . . . . . . . . . 19
The Horror Begins to Unfold . . . . . . . . . . . . . . . . . . 36
The Downward Spiral Begins . . . . . . . . . . . . . . . . . 50
The Truth Revealed . . . . . . . . . . . . . . . . . . . . . . . . 59
The Air I Breathe . . . . . . . . . . . . . . . . . . . . . . . . . 138
A Mother's Message . . . . . . . . . . . . . . . . . . . . . . 140
Resources . . . . . . . . . . . . . . . . . . . . . . . . . . . . . 143

# Acknowledgments

I am grateful to my friends and family who supported me during difficult times while I uncovered the truth about my past 30 years of life.

I extend my thanks to my daughter for her inner strength, for allowing me to see myself through her eyes, and for the love she offers, which brings me a sense of comfort.

I am grateful to Ginger for her patience and unwavering faith in me over the years. Her kind heart gave me the courage to face my fears and complete this project.

I am blessed to have been raised by a father, who taught me the value of strength, generosity, and perseverance to accomplish anything I put my mind to.

Thank you, God, for providing me with the fortitude I needed to safeguard my children and keep them surrounded by good people who showed them only love.

*A mother I was,*
*A mother I will always be.*
*Like a lioness that protects her cubs,*
*At all costs,*
*And against all odds.*
—Alice Nehme

# THE STORY

I can't get the images out of my head. It was a Cinderella story, a true nightmare, and a living horror that took and framed the last 34 years of my life.

We met in high school in 1984. I was 17 and he was 19. Thirty-four years later, he was dead.

My son called me on July 25, 2022, as I was about to leave the house to head over to my aunt's home for a family dinner. He called to say his sister was on her way, and that we had to have an immediate family meeting.

He showed up with his wife, pregnant with their first child, to announce his father's death.

I couldn't distinguish between sadness, relief, or fear of what my children were about to go through. My daughter drove home frantically and as she got out of the car, she started screaming. "What is it! I know something is wrong!"

I spent the last 34 years struggling and protecting my children from a lot of things that went on while being blamed by his family for not allowing him to see the children. His mother did nothing to ensure the wellbeing of her grandchildren. What mother allows this? She sat in her glass house, living a life of luxury while the children barely had enough food because he spent all the money in our bank accounts.

I never understood "why". Why did he walk out on me and the children in January of 2001, and why did he torment us for years — until I had him arrested so it would stop. I knew he smoked marijuana in his younger days, but I honestly thought it was an occasional thing.

I was wrong.

I had no idea about the truth. We went inside the house, numb with emotion as my son started showing me text messages from his aunt who was giving him the run around about entering the apartment where they found the body, and drugs on his stove top.

We had suspected they were hiding something and then we learned they had emptied a lot of the content in the apartment.

After several days they finally allowed him to enter. He immediately noticed many things were missing.

With a look of fear, my son said to me, "Mom, there is a journal dad wrote while in rehab."

My heart dropped to the floor, and I felt sick to my stomach. I knew my life would be in there and the confessions would be my answers.

His family started giving the children a difficult time, and sent an email to my daughter, saying,

"I imagine since you wanted nothing to do with your father for most of your life then I will also assume you will hold to your high standards and want nothing from his apartment."

They tried to control the estate and one of his sisters had taken his computer out of the apartment and deleted all the data, therefore having tampered with it.

Once again, the attacks started on my daughter, who had been traumatized by her father. He had locked her in a room. That day was the final straw; the thing that finally made the courts remove his right to visitation with the children. She hadn't seen him for the last 20 years.

Following the messages back and forth that my son was having with his father's family, I saw exactly where this was going to go.

I called my lawyer and asked him to come to the house to meet with me and the children. There was no way I was going to relive this horror and allow this family to point any more fingers. I was putting a stop to this before it got out of hand.

I went into my filing cabinet and pulled out the six-inch-thick divorce file that dragged on for 10 years, and my lioness claws came out to protect my children. That's all I did for 32 years was protect, protect, and protect. I had no peace.

This file had police reports, hospital reports, child services reports, psychosocial expertise, and all the abuse, anxiety, and terror I lived through until 2011.

I said, "As God is my witness, they will not touch my children."

As terrified as I was, I asked my son to bring me the journal. His father had to write it as his therapy and treatment from the day he started rehab on May 11, 2011, 10 years after he walked out on us.

After writing my book on drug addiction in 2010, I found out he bought it, called the drug rehab placement specialist, who wrote a testimonial for my book, and admitted himself into rehab. How ironic that my first book on addiction called, *A Testimonial of Insanity*, was what made him get help. He told the rehab specialist that he realized what he had done to his mother and the pain he put her through. Something every child should learn and never dishonor a mother nor their upbringing.

While in my kitchen, waiting for our attorney to arrive, I flipped through the pages and started to scream, while reading his confessions. I thought I was going to collapse. The children ran to me and tried to calm me down. The horror had just begun to unfold and all I could say was, "God help me."

# The Beginning

We met in high school. It was 1984. He was a quiet boy sitting at the back of the classroom. We both went to the same private school; a prep school located in Montreal.

Being as shy as he was, he eventually joined our group of friends and used to hang out with us on a daily basis. One day he invited me to his mother's penthouse, which was located in Westmount Square on two floors occupying 4,000 square feet of luxury, decorated by the renowned Claude Hinton designer in Montreal. I remember driving there the first time during our lunch break from school.

As we entered the Westmount Square underground parking lot, it smelt of toast and butter.

We parked in the underground garage, then went upstairs into the penthouse, and as we opened the large doors, my mouth dropped to the floor.

I had never seen a penthouse so big, on two floors, with wall-to-wall windows overlooking the city.

I remember him telling me that he wasn't allowed to take his mother's car. He took her Mazda sports car back-and-forth to school. Sure enough he had a fender bender and damaged her front bumper, but made sure to have it repaired before she returned from Florida.

# The Beginning

We used to have lunch at Franni's café around the corner from school where I would typically have a quiche with a salad, and then one of their famous cheesecakes.

They made the best cheesecakes in Montreal and were quite well-known. I have fond memories of that place that unfortunately no longer exists today.

I was voted president of the student council, and a popular kid. One day, he asked me to go out with him. We started to date, and things seemed normal back then.

We had a lot of school friends, all from families with money. As teenagers we never lacked the means to eat in restaurants.

We used to go to a restaurant called Casa Napoli in the Italian district of Montreal. We would often see Italian groups there having dinner and clearly conducting business conversations. Coming from the types of families we came from this wasn't an unusual thing to see. My father was an influential person in the Lebanese community.

The end of the school year arrived really quickly, and all of our friends went onto their summer vacations, planning for the next step which would be college. We had prom and then everyone began summer vacation. High school was finished, a new phase of life was beginning.

Soon afterwards, his mother was to be remarried. He asked me if I would go with him to her wedding. Coming from an old-fashioned and very strict upbringing, I started to panic trying to figure out how I was going to ask my father if I could go to this wedding as his date.

To avoid conflict, I told my mother about it, and asked her to find a way to tell my father.

My father came up to me and asked me who this boy was. I said, "Dad, it's just a boy from school who wanted to bring me to his mother's wedding. I will drive there and come back on my own."

My father agreed.

I needed an outfit, so my mother took me to a boutique in the shopping center where I bought myself an off-white Gianfranco

Ferre skirt suit. I wore an orange hat and matching orange high heeled shoes for the occasion.

I met him at the church, parked my car and went inside. After the ceremony we headed to the reception hall to have dinner and celebrate the day. I started to notice he was getting more and more drunk and that's where I told him it was time to go and that I would drive him home.

I could see that he was depressed and shared that his father had commit suicide and now his mother got remarried. He was really troubled and screwed up by the event. Being only 17, and him 19, I didn't really think this would be a lifetime problem or a mental situation that would destroy us.

We arrived at his apartment. I walked him up to his room, laid him down on his bed, and that was when he started pulling me towards him, as I said no. He then proceeded to call me a whore and treat me like garbage. I ran out of there so fast and went home. I wanted nothing to do with him and never told anyone about what happened as it would have been a shame to repeat what he did. The next day I ignored his calls and continued to ignore him until he got the message.

That summer I decided to visit my cousin in Florida. My mother bought me my airline ticket and set me off to spend two weeks enjoying a vacation. On my return flight, I sat in the long rows that were basically empty. There was a boy at the end of the aisle, who said hello to me. We introduced ourselves and started talking, which kept us busy for our flight back.

A couple of days later I showed up at my first day in College. It was orientation and registration day. We were to select our classes and prepare for the start of school. It was an exciting time as we entered into a new cycle of life.

I suddenly felt a tap on my shoulder. There he was, that boy from the end of the aisle in the plane. He looked at me and said, "this must be fate."

I laughed and we exchanged phone numbers. We dated for about eight months. He was very kind and very polite and always very respectful. His father worked in a factory and his mother was a cleaning lady. He studied hard and had a strong ambition to become successful.

His mother would invite me for dinner every week, as my mother did in return. Whenever I ate at their house, she always made me her macaroni salad that I loved. Still today, I make it the same way and always think of her.

A few months into our dating, my ex kept lurking around the house and trying to get my attention.

I would see him drive by and sit outside the house as I basically ignored him. One day he came and knocked on the door and said, "Can we please speak? " I'm not sure why I allowed him to speak to me after what he did but I know that, much younger, I was quite forgiving, and felt that I could save the world. Clearly, I now know I made a huge mistake. People don't change and bad characters only worsen.

He begged me to give him a chance. My mother never quite accepted the boy from the plane.

My family was a prominent Lebanese family in Montreal, so I felt this obligation to go in a different direction so that my parents wouldn't be disappointed.

I decided to give my ex a chance and told the boy from the plane that I couldn't see him anymore. I was so sad, knowing I had broken his heart. Today I wonder what would have been had I chosen a different path.

About 10 years ago, we reconnected and remained friends. I respect him a lot and have fond memories from our teen years.

Shortly afterwards, my ex asked me to marry him. Somehow my father, who didn't accept anyone, accepted him for some reason, even though he wasn't Lebanese and didn't come from our culture. His grandfather's brother was married to a Lebanese woman my family knew, so I guess it made more sense to them at the time.

We got engaged, and the wedding plans began. We booked the church, the reception hall, the band and started planning for the big day. The chosen date was the 28th of August 1988.

I had wanted a dress similar to that of Princess Diana when she married Prince Charles. Back in the 80's, it was very popular to have long puffy sleeves and big shoulders. I laugh today at the ridiculous styles we had in the disco era.

My mother and I chose the best satin and lace. The dress weighed a ton, with a big crinoline under the skirt and a very long train.

A renowned Lebanese dress maker made the dress to custom fit my tiny body and sewed every single pearl one by one on each part of the lace. It took her months to finish.

My bridesmaids wore teal colors and also every dress was custom sewn. They were all so beautiful.

Coming from a very big family, my mother was excited and started planning the wedding shower. All our family and friends attended. It was almost like being in My Big Fat Greek Wedding, but Lebanese style.

I arrived at my wedding shower to find hundreds of wrapped gifts. Everything under the sun was in that room. I basically had nothing to buy starting married life. Anything and everything was wrapped in those boxes. We had a grand time with about 150 women.

My father paid for this wedding and left nothing out. It was the wedding of the decade.

We ordered the invitations and 350 invites went out by mail. There was a lot of writing back then to fill out names and addresses.

We decided to rent our first apartment together and get it ready for me to move into after the wedding. Coming from a strict middle eastern family, of course I wasn't allowed to live with a man unless we were married. Our traditions and community didn't accept such a thing. I never really knew what it was to live with him under the same roof. He gave notice to his current apartment, and we packed up and moved into the new place. My mother bought us our bedroom set and dining room which I still have today. It was very modern but timeless and still looks great.

## The Beginning

All the furniture came from an Italian manufacturer on the east side of Montreal. It was all custom made to our liking. Our first couch was a beautiful Italian sectional that was so comfortable. We bought our first giant screen television when they had just come out. It was a 60-inch rear projection TV made by Pioneer, with a surround sound system to go with it. All our draperies were made to measure by my family who own a very big textile business.

I had chosen my bridal registry at Linen Chest where they had the finest of dishware and kitchenware back then. Today it is very different.

The big day arrived quickly, and as I drove in my car, I started to feel a terrible sensation in my stomach. I pulled over and decided to call my father to say, "Dad, there's something wrong, something doesn't feel right. I don't know if I should be getting married."

My father said to me, "My daughter, it's normal to have cold feet before a wedding. Everyone is coming, your grandmother is flying in from the Middle East, you're just having cold feet, it'll all be okay."

That week my grandmother flew in from Beirut to attend my wedding. I showed up at our new apartment and waited for him so we could drive to the airport together and meet my family who would be there to greet my grandmother.

As he stepped into the apartment he was drunk and stoned. I was in shock and disgusted and now in a panic. How could he show up at the airport in this state? The anxiety I still live with today all began that day. I was so young, so naive thinking I could change him.

The day arrived. Everyone was at my parents' house. It was filled with family and friends, as I was getting ready. The hairdresser was there, the limousines arrived, and as I was putting on my dress and having my hair done while people were serving food to all of the guests in the house. The guests came to me one by one to give me a kiss and wish me well. I was like a princess sitting on a throne as everyone walked up to me.

The photographer was snapping photos nonstop and capturing the moments that I would have for life. So many people were walking in to our home, the home I was about to leave.

The moment arrived. I stood up after having my hair done to perfection surrounded by my bridesmaids and family members who lifted up my train as we walked down the stairs towards the limousines that waited outside.

My father opened the door with pride and helped me into the car. We drove to the church, with a long procession behind us as everybody honked their horns in the streets celebrating the big day. It began to rain, and I started to feel like it was an omen. As the saying goes, it's typically bad luck when it rains on your wedding day.

We arrived at the church. They pulled out umbrellas as my father covered me and walked with me up the stairs to the front doors. The church was filled with flowers and ribbons on every pew. There were 350 people sitting and waiting for me to arrive. The doors opened as my father and I waited with my mother by his side. My mother walked down the aisle to the front pew on the left side of the altar and turned around as she waited for me to appear. The bridesmaids followed one by one carrying their beautiful bouquets to stand alongside the altar.

As I stepped forward,there he was, my future husband, waiting at the front altar in his black tuxedo. Father Anthony looked at me and smiled as he was around for my birth, my baptism, and now my wedding. He recently passed away after having been the longest reigning priest, serving 50 years at the St. George Orthodox Church.

The ceremony began as I walked down the aisle with my father, proud to give me away. He gave me a kiss on the forehead and wished me well.

Little did we know then that he was handing me over to the devil.

The ceremony began. It lasted about an hour and a half with a choir singing prayers reading passages from the Bible and the wedding having been the traditional Greek orthodox ceremony with the changing of the crowns.

We were finally wed as we signed our names on the marital licenses in the church.

Everyone clapped and hollered, enjoying themselves as we walked out of the church to get back into the limousines. Of course, everybody threw confetti. I even found some in my underwear at the end of the night.

We proceeded to the Hilton hotel where we were hosting a reception in the grand ballroom seating 350 people, with the biggest most popular band in the city named Paul Chakra and the 1945 band.

We arrived at the hotel for cocktails. As the guests enjoyed their drinks and hors d'oeuvres, we proceeded to have the picture session with the photographers and videographers.

As I look back at my wedding album today, I am sad to see *all of* the people who are no longer with us, but at the same time, it warms my heart to see my father and mother and family members who have since passed away.

Although life became a horror soon afterwards, at least I had memories of my parents from those pictures and videos.

The ballroom was full as everybody waited for us. There we were, entering the grand ballroom, as everyone clapped while the band played music and announced us as husband and wife. We had the best band in the city. It was the "1945 Band." They were exceptional.

We proceeded to the head table to find my mother and father, my mother-in-law and her husband, my maid of honor and his brother, the best man.

The evening was a success, as all of my cousins' played jokes, and made it a very festive celebration. The band was entertaining, the choice of music was amazing, and the food was of course exceptional.

Everyone danced all night, and we had a wonderful memorable day all around. As the night started to wind down, and they brought out the dessert tables, I went back to the honeymoon suite and changed into a more comfortable evening dress.

It was time to bring out the wedding cake. We had ordered a six-tier cake from Patisserie Gascogne that was absolutely splendid. This pastry shop was renowned and made exquisite French pastries and cakes. After 60 years in operation, the upscale pastry shop closed its doors and put 175 people in the Montreal region out of work on January 5, 2018, 20 years after our wedding.

We proceeded to cut the wedding cake as they put out tables and tables of French pastries and Lebanese pastries to complete the evening. The night started to reach an end, and everyone went home while we went back to our honeymoon suite to prepare for our next morning departure to the beautiful islands of Greece.

The next morning, I woke up to find my entire family joining us for breakfast at the hotel before our trip.

My mother came up to me and asked me how I was. I started to laugh as I understood where she was going with that question because, back then, in our Lebanese culture, a young girl was supposed to remain a virgin until she got married.

We proceeded to go into the dining rooms and have breakfast with the entire family. It was lovely to see everyone before we left on our honeymoon. Once breakfast was over my father drove us to the airport in his Chrysler Le baron as we unloaded our luggage and prepared for a three-week trip in beautiful Greece.

We headed to the airport terminal all excited and couldn't wait to get onto the plane. Our flight was with KLM on August 29,1988.

We boarded the plane, sat in our seats, and settled in as we anxiously awaited take-off.

After several hours in the air, I started to feel the plane jumping up and down due to turbulence. The pilot announced that we would be entering a very heavy storm zone. Although I was never afraid of flying, having flown with my father in his private plane and also having about 100 hours of flying time myself to

## The Beginning

get my pilot's license. I wasn't too nervous but did start to feel a bit shaky and worried.

At this time the stewardesses were serving dinner. Our dinner plates arrived, and we began to eat. Suddenly, the plane dropped sharply, and our plates and cups went flying into the air. It was like a movie scene. Passengers were screaming and anticipating the worst.

I turned and looked at my husband and said,"I think we're going to die."

It seemed like hours of trembling and anxiety before the plane finally exited the storm and we were relieved that it was over. I was shaken up, but all was well, and we arrived in Amsterdam safe and sound.

Next, we needed to catch our connecting flight to Athens. As we waited, I was quite nervous, but the layover allowed us to calm down before getting on the next plane. It was time to embark on the flight to Athens Greece. This flight was smooth and there were no issues, so I felt much better.

We arrived in Greece, got a taxi cab, and proceeded to our hotel in the center of Athens. We spent three days in Athens before beginning our island hopping around the Greek Islands. Our first hotel was right across from the Grand Bretagne in the center of town where you would find restaurants and outdoor patios to sit and enjoy a meal and drinks.

Little did we know that we would meet a couple who were also on their honeymoon and end up becoming lifetime friends.

We spent the first day touring the island visiting orthodox churches, museums, and different sites. We rented a scooter to get around which was a lot of fun but actually quite dangerous. Their scooters weren't really well maintained and seemed old and rundown but ours served our purpose to zoom around and discover things.

That day we headed out to see the Parthenon which was also quite rundown, and its ruins were in need of some loving restoration. I think it's been rebuilt since then. We had gone around basically picking up something to eat along the way. The next day we did some more sightseeing and decided to eat in the outdoor courtyard in front of our hotel.

That day I ordered a cheeseburger and French fries. As the cheeseburger arrived at my table, I lifted up the top bun to add some condiments and noticed that the meat was of a greenish color. I got quite disgusted and decided to take the meat patty out of the bun and feed it to the cats who were lurking around in the courtyard. They were sitting right next to us, our future lifetime friends, Jeff and Cathy, from Connecticut who were also on their honeymoon.

We exchanged phone numbers as our itineraries were very different so we knew we wouldn't be seeing them during our three weeks in Greece. The next day after having a green hamburger I decided to ask the hotel to recommend the best restaurant in Athens. They told us to go eat at a restaurant called Myrtia. I was looking forward to it and at the end of the day we returned to our hotel to take a shower and get ready for our dinner.

Somebody had sabotaged the power plant in the city and everything and everyone lost power that day including the elevators in our hotel. Our room was on the 16th floor.

After getting showered and dressed we headed down the stairs, to the reception desk and asked them to call the restaurant. It was impossible given the power outage.

We headed out regardless and took a chance hoping it would still be open. As we arrived there we were greeted by a lovely gentleman. We asked him if the restaurant was open given there was no electricity. He answered, "Yes." So, I then asked if he would be able to cook anything from the menu. He looked at me and said, " Madam, do you trust me?" I answered, "I suppose so."

We entered the restaurant. It was getting dark as the sun was setting and they brought us wonderful plates one after another. I don't quite remember everything we ate but what I do remember is that there were lots of different grilled meats and the food was absolutely fantastic. It is a place I will never forget.

Our few days in Athens were coming to an end. We packed up and got ready for the next part of the trip. We took a taxi to the

## The Beginning

airport where we got on our flight to take us out to the island of Mykonos.

We arrived in Mykonos and flagged a taxi to take us to our rental apartment. Then we got onto a shuttle which took us to a beach. When we arrived at the beach, we started to walk down the sand and settle into an area in front of the ocean. As I started to look around, I saw nothing but nude people walking up and down the beach. I was a little confused and turned to my husband and said, "Are we are on a nude beach?"

I started to laugh sitting there in my beautiful white bikini as people were looking at us as if we were the strange ones. I was quite uncomfortable, but I think I was most uncomfortable with people looking at us like we were weird. I lay down on my back and took off the top part of my bikini but didn't move. I was uncomfortable taking off the bottom so basically, I just stayed topless. At some point it was so hot, I got up and walked into the ocean and realized that nobody was even looking at me. It's amazing how situations can just sensitize you or desensitize you depending on where you are and who you are with. The next day we made sure to go to a beach that wasn't a nudist beach.

WE ENJOYED OUR stay in Mykonos and then started our adventure on Paros and then we were off to the final island of Santorini.

We got to the airport in Mykonos, checked in our bags and went through the gates heading towards the runway to our plane. As we stepped outside onto the runway. I looked at my husband and said, "Oh my God, look at how old that plane is. It almost looks like one of the Wright brothers' planes."

Next thing I knew they were leading us up to that plane and I couldn't believe we were actually getting on. We climbed the ladder and got on the aircraft to find only one row of seats where everyone sat one behind the other. The plane took off and as scared as I was, I just held on tight.

As we were approaching the island of Santorini, I noticed our plane was landing on the top of the cliff, actually the rim of the volcano, on a very narrow runway. That in itself was terrifying. As the plane touched down, I held my breath because it seemed as though we had no room on that narrow runway. I felt as though we could glide right off that cliff. Crazy as it seems, we were completely fine.

The island of Santorini was built up by layers of lava created by volcanic eruptions, and it had experienced three significant eruptions that formed overlapping calderas or collapsed magma chambers. The natural and man-made beauty of Santorini comes from the unique circumstance in which the island as we know it was made during the second millennium BC, around 3000 years ago. A huge volcanic eruption, one of the largest in recorded history, dramatically altered the shape of the Island. Today, it is one of the most beautiful islands in the world. It is absolutely breathtaking and is a place I would definitely visit over and over again. I don't think I could ever get bored of visiting Santorini.

We rented a scooter again on the island in order to be able to visit all the different beaches and touristic sites. We had the opportunity to swim in the Hot Springs at the bottom of the volcanoes where the water was warm. We also travelled to the different beaches where we found some beaches with black sand and others with red sand.

I was absolutely taken away by the Candlemas Orthodox Cathedral located at the top of the cliff. The view was breath-taking. In my opinion, it is one of the most incredible sites in the world. I found myself just staring in awe at every hand-painted and etched piece on every wall, creating unforgettable memories.

One night we ate at a restaurant by the name of Zorba's located at the top of the cliff. Sitting there, I looked up at the ceiling to find octopus hanging on ropes above our heads. It was quite something to see.

The Greeks are known for their grilled octopus plates, savored with spices and a texture only they have perfected. Of course,

## The Beginning

being there dining on freshly caught octopus can never compare to the ones we eat back home.

I then got up from my seat and looked over the side of the cliff to find the most beautiful cruise liner docked at the beach below our restaurant. It was the Sea Goddess 1. It was so magnificent, I decided to walk down the very long set of steps to the beach and look at it up close. *It was my dream to cruise on this luxury liner, and I always said that one day I would do it. It caters to only 116 guests and each cabin is a luxury room.*

The Sea Goddess line had planned to build eight identical luxury ships, however, before the program was completed the company faced financial trouble. Because of that, only two of the vessels were completed. The first vessel was Sea Goddess 1 which entered service in 1984. Cunard line acquired management rights to these ships and formed the Cunard Sea Goddess brand which was created to operate these two unique vessels.

*As I sit here in Barbados, writing this book and doing research about the Sea Goddess, I discovered that right here in front of me at the port of Bridgetown is exactly where the Sea Goddess lies. The reason I didn't know this is that they have changed the name since then to "Sea Dream" one who is now run by the princess cruise lines. Cunard cruise lines had sold it to them after spending approximately 30 years running the ships. So, I have contacted my travel agent and asked her to book me a six-day cruise on this lovely luxury liner that I've always wanted to go on for next January when I return to Barbados.*

AFTER THREE BEAUTIFUL weeks in Greece, it was time to go home. And although I felt safe and happy in Greece, I knew it was time to return, but I wasn't looking forward to the flight home.

We gathered our belongings and headed to the airport. We flew back from Santorini to Athens on a connecting flight back to Amsterdam and then back to Montreal. The flight was smooth with no issues for our return. I was happy to be home. No matter how much I travel, there is no place like home.

# MARRIED LIFE BEGINS

Married life was about to begin. We had rented a two-bedroom, corner apartment with a view of the city. *Having lived at home under my mother's cooking, I never really learned much in regard to the kitchen. Today, I have extensive experience in restoration having owned a pasta factory and catering business—I am a master in pasta making. To this day, I still run a small online food business.*

We arrived home and it was time to go to the grocery store. I walked through there, completely lost, having no idea what to buy. I went through the meat section, bought some ground beef, and then headed to the spice section. I tried to get creative by reading the different types of spices that were available. I picked up a package of sloppy Joe mix and read the back. I had to find some hamburger buns. That was going to be our dinner. I headed home and read the instructions, fried up the meat with the sloppy Joe mixed together in the pan, poured it onto the hamburger bun, and dinner was served. It didn't take me long to learn how to cook by doing a lot of reading and following recipes in cookbooks.

WE SPENT ABOUT seven months in this apartment while looking for a house. We found a beautiful three-bedroom house across the street from the river and bought it in May of 1989, while pregnant with my first child. I worked hard trying to decorate it and make it our own. We had just enough for the purchase of the house. We moved in with our bedroom set and dining room and living room furniture. The rest of the house had to be furnished so slowly. We started a budget in order to be able to complete furnishing the rest. It was a tight budget every week, so that we could manage the bills and save as quickly as possible in order to buy the baby furniture and complete some rooms in the house.

When we announced the pregnancy to my mother-in-law, her response was, "I'm not ready to be a grandmother." When I announced the news to my parents, they cried and were ecstatically happy.

My pregnancy was difficult in the beginning. I had a lot of nausea and morning sickness. I remember not even being able to walk into a supermarket by the meat counter. I would start gagging. Even just the smell of cut grass outside would make me throw up. I basically spent the first five months eating soda crackers, and pieces of cheese just to try to get something into my stomach.

By the fifth month, I started to feel better and that's when the all dressed pizzas kicked in. I would eat an entire large pie all by myself. Having been an athlete, I got married and only weighed about 102 pounds. By the time I gave birth to my first child I only weighed 124 pounds.

Around the sixth month into my pregnancy, we decided to go to Disney World in Orlando, Florida. I have always been a lover of Disney and Mickey Mouse. I'm a kid when it comes to Disney. I go crazy with excitement whenever I am near Disney.

## Married Life Begins

As an adult, anytime I have been near a Disney store, I run into the store and don't even know who I am with anymore. My daughter laughs and just watches me go.

We had so much fun. During the vacation, it was like being in a dream every day, in awe, watching the parades and going on the rides. Of course, I would just freeze when I saw Mickey.

After a wonderful time at Disney, it was time to go home and settle in while we waited for the baby to arrive.

WINTER CAME AND I was home waiting to give birth to my little angel. He started working for my father's company. One day I received an envelope in the mail. It was a loan for a skidoo. As I stared at it, I couldn't understand what this was about because we were trying to live on a strict budget since we were starting a family and needed every cent possible to get ready for the baby.

He came home that night, and I confronted him as I held this piece of paper in front of him. He looked at me and didn't have anything to say. I asked him what this was. He simply stated that he bought a skidoo. I was furious with him. He was never really responsible with money and used to do things that didn't make any sense. Afterall, we were trying to live within our means and were just starting out with a baby on her way. We didn't even have much furniture in the house, yet he went out and bought a skidoo!? I thought I could take charge of the finances and that things would be under control, but in reality, that never happened because he was out of control.

I told my father about it, and he said, "So, that explains why he comes in to work late and his face is red from the cold outside." Now, I was even more disgusted knowing he didn't even get to work on time. He was taking advantage of my father's generosity. My father never even told me anything. He just patiently accepted his behavior.

I told him he had to sell the skidoo. We certainly didn't need to keep paying for a loan. This wasn't the time for such an expense.

The bad thing about it all is, he never insured the vehicle. One day the skidoo got stolen and because he hadn't insured it, we had to continue paying for the loan. Now that I think about it, I wonder if that too was a lie and he just said it wasn't insured so he could keep using it and hide it from me, given we still had to pay the loan regardless.

AFTER THAT INCIDENT, I started to feel unsafe with him and realized he was a liar and a manipulator. Here I was trapped in my life and didn't know what to do. So, I went through day after day in denial, with a baby, hoping things would improve.

This is when my anxiety became stifling, and I started to suspect things. I didn't trust what was going on or believe anything he had to say.

One day I decided to go look in his car, opened up the trunk to search for any more things that I may not have known about. What did I find? A trunk full of porn magazines.

Coming from a proper family, this was something that totally shocked me. I confronted him about it and his answer to me was, "I like this." I was so furious at him that I took the magazines and threw them at him. I didn't know back then what was really going on. Back then I just tried to ignore it hoping it would stop and he would grow up. Here I was nine months pregnant waiting to expect our first child, and I really felt uncomfortable in this marriage. At this point, I couldn't even tell my parents what was going on. They were raised with old-fashioned beliefs from the Middle East, and I was ashamed to even bring up something of the sort. So, I just kept quiet and tried to manage life on my own.

# Married Life Begins

IT WAS DECEMBER 20, 1989, when motherhood began for me. I went into labor, and that day was one of the biggest snowstorms recorded in the history of Montreal. It was so bad that they closed the main highway into the city. We got into our Toyota 4Runner, 4 x 4, and started our journey to the hospital.

As we approached the entrance of the highway, the police had barricaded the entrance so that no one could drive onto it. We pulled over and rolled down my window next to a police officer who was standing outside and said, "We can handle the snow with this truck. I'm in labor and have to get to the hospital immediately."

The police officer turned around and waved to his partner, instructing him to open up the entrance to the highway. We found ourselves driving down to the Jewish General hospital in Montreal by ourselves with no one else on the road.

When we arrived, my doctor was patiently waiting for me. After looking at me and analyzing as to why I wasn't dilating, he decided to do an examination only to discover the baby was breech. He immediately ordered an emergency C-section because my baby was starting to lose oxygen.

They rolled me down to the emergency room at such a high speed they dashed through the hallway and into the elevator. They even shaved me while we were in the elevator heading down to the ER.

I then heard my doctor say, "Get a spinal, we gotta get this baby out!"

They turned me over onto my side and injected me with a spinal needle that literally put me to sleep within seconds. He asked me to count backwards from ten and as I started the countdown, I got to about seven and I was out.

Apparently, they did an emergency C-section, pulled her out and she was fine. When I woke up in recovery, my last memory was that everyone was in a panic. I had no idea if the baby was okay. I was struggling to wake up, fighting the anesthetic, and remembering having said, "Where's my baby? Is it a girl or a boy?" They told me it was a girl, so I asked if she was okay, and requested they bring her to me.

As soon as I was able, they brought her to me, and I immediately started nursing her for the first time. That feeling of being a mother and the enormous love I felt never stopped from that day on.

I SPENT FIVE days in the hospital and went home to my new life on December 25, Christmas Day. It was my best Christmas gift ever, my baby girl. Everyone was so excited, especially my parents.

My father had gone shopping at the Hudson's Bay Department store right after Christmas Day and there sitting on the Christmas display was a burgundy checkered miniature armchair measuring 18 inches high and 12 inches wide. He asked the saleswoman how much they wanted for the chair. The woman replied that it wasn't for sale. That had to be the funniest thing I heard. She obviously didn't know who my father was. It would be like telling Don Corleon he can't buy the chair.

My doorbell rang and there he was, the proudest grandfather (*Geddo*) holding that miniature armchair in his hands standing with a smile on his face and tears of joy in his eyes.

My children were his world, and he did anything and everything for them. I always let him do as he wished with them so he could be the grandfather he chose to be. I believed in letting him enjoy grandfather-hood the way he wanted to.

The first night after breastfeeding and putting her down in her crib, I fell asleep after a long six days of recuperating from the caesarean section and lack of sleep. The morning showed up faster than ever and I jumped out of bed realizing she never woke up during the night. I was terrified thinking something was wrong. I walked quickly, hunched over in pain, to get to her room.

There she lay with her pacifier in her mouth, and not a sound from that little angel. In fact, she never said a peep, not even with a full diaper. She was a happy and easy baby and slept through the night from day one. I quickly realized that my aunts who gave me instructions on perfect mothering skills obviously worked.

1. Feed her every three hours sharp, not before, not after, for the first 40 days then remove the middle of the night feeding.

2. Always let her sleep in her own bed for every nap (if I was home) and every night's sleep. She should learn to be alone in her bed and breathe her own fresh air.

I lucked out as the baby followed my lead. She is still a lover of sleep and craves her bed even as an adult.

Things were stable for a while. I didn't really sense anything. I was too occupied with the baby and having lunch and shopping dates with family and friends.

I got the baby used to noise, seeing people, and going around. We were equipped with the best and most practical things.

Every day we ate dinner with my aunt and uncle—one day at our house and the next day at their house. I would put the baby in a portable playpen where she was safe, happy, played with toys and slept, having never complained about anything. I loved spending every possible minute with her.

IN DECEMBER OF 1990, we flew to Miami to spend Christmas with our grandparents-in-law. They owned a hotel in Miami and offered us an apartment to stay in. I always, always, loved seeing them. They were a classy and kind couple who showed me nothing but love. They were thrilled to be great grandparents.

My daughter loved being in the ocean and playing on the beach. She was the cutest thing ever and constantly had a smile on her face. She was the first grandchild on both sides and certainly got spoiled.

LIFE CONTINUED AND soon afterwards I was pregnant with my son. Both babies had the same due date in December, my daughter was born on the 20th and my son the 8th. He was much bigger than my daughter was. She was 6 lbs. 11 oz. while my son was an unexpected 8lbs. 1oz. He was a little more difficult, at first, than my daughter was but it took about five days to train his sleep habits and voila, a model baby. I was able to give birth naturally this time with no complications.

People called me the "Baby Whisperer". I have a way with children, my mother always told me this. The children slept through the night from the day they came home from the hospital and never really experienced any colic or much discomfort. I had the skills for everything I needed, so that I wouldn't have any issues. No colic, no diaper rash, nothing to battle.

We enjoyed time with our friends and family in our home and would visit our friends in Connecticut every 2–3 weeks. Life was fun and full of adventures.

THE NEXT SUMMER, we had an in-ground pool built with a diving board in order to enjoy the summers to the fullest. The area was beautiful as we took long walks along the river.

That summer we bought a 17-foot boat and docked it at the marina just down the street from our home. We had a lot of fun taking it out for rides in the summer with our family and friends.

One day we were sitting outside by our pool and my in-laws came over to spend the day with us and have a BBQ. My ex decided to go out to the store and instead of taking his car he took his sister's car that was parked behind him.

Upon his return, he told us he had been in an accident, having hit a parked car around the corner from us. I couldn't understand how he managed to drive into a parked car. *In fact, when I think about it now, he often had fender benders which didn't make sense.*

WE LIVED IN that house for about two years until after my son was born. We both hated the winter and contemplated moving to South Florida. My ex had lived there with his family when he was young, so it was familiar to him. I also visited Florida many, many times over my life and loved the ocean and being in the sun. So, we decided to put our house up for sale and head down to South Florida to give it a try.

The house sold very quickly, and we basically recovered any investment we had put into it. After we closed on the house we packed our bags. We got a moving company to pack up our furniture and headed to Florida.

On our way, we decided to stop in New York and spend some time visiting the city. We booked a suite at The Waldorf and drove both our cars given it was the easiest way to get them there.

New York was fun, and we took the children to FAO Schwarz. They spent hours and hours playing. It was amazing just to see the glow upon their little faces. They were always happy children.

After about five days, we continued our travel heading south. Given we weren't in a rush and had the children with us, and two cars, we clearly took our time, stopping often along the way.

When we arrived in Miami, we didn't have a place to live yet, so we spent the first few months living in my grandfather-in-law's hotel in Bal Harbour. They gave us a beautiful apartment to use and day after day we drove around, trying to decide which community we would settle in that was best to raise children surrounded by quality schools and families.

Back then there were no computers, so the internet wasn't available to help on our search. We started driving around and as we got to Yamato Road, in Boca Raton, we got off the highway and headed West.

We passed a community called The Broken Sound Country Club, which looked beautiful, so we stopped in to inquire about the homes. Along that road there was a man taking care of the grass in the middle of the street. I noticed the grass going from yellow to green and said, "Wow, look at that! That must be some unbelievable fertilizer. It's turning the grass green instantaneously. "Little did I know how silly that statement was. The man that was taking care of the grass was actually painting it!

We entered the country club and asked to speak with a real estate agent to see some of the properties. We fell upon a lovely couple from New York who were working there. They took us around to see some homes and gave us prices, but we quickly realized that it was much too expensive for us and not within our immediate budget.

Roy, the real estate agent, suggested we go next-door to visit the Woodfield Country Club. It was a beautiful community that had gone into bankruptcy during construction and was taken over by the RTC who decided to continue the project. Because it was coming out of bankruptcy the homes were better priced. We visited a community called Victoria isles, where they were building three- and four-bedroom homes. I fell in love with a bungalow there, which was a three-bedroom/two-bathroom home.

As I looked at the plans, I decided to ask if we could extend the house to add a fourth bedroom and a third bathroom. They didn't charge us much to modify the plan, so we felt good about the decision to sign the paperwork.

Construction was supposed to take about four to six months. So temporarily, we decided to rent an apartment nearby so we could keep an eye on the project and start getting used to the surroundings.

I used to go pretty much every day to check on the construction and see how things were progressing. It was a lot of fun to get to pick kitchen cabinets, flooring, appliances, carpets, and the color of paint for the walls.

The project went along pretty well. One day, I entered the house when they were receiving the appliances for the kitchen. All of 118 pounds of me walked into that kitchen that day and the man installing the appliances looked at me and asked, "Can I help you?"

I answered, "I'm the owner of the house, just coming to see how things are coming along."

He looked at me and asked, "You're the owner of the house?"

"Yes."

He told me he thought it would be some big Italian lady who had designed this kitchen with two ovens, a Jenn-air cooktop, and large counters. I started to laugh. "No, just a small 118-pound Lebanese woman."

The construction came along very nicely, and soon enough we found ourselves moving into our first home in South Florida.

We were still distributing my father's textiles. My ex-husband would go down to Miami to look for clients … so I thought. We lived in a country club, and the children had a lot of fun with the neighboring families.

We spent many years hanging out at the country club by the pool. The children would show up at the tiki bar and order their ice cream on our food and beverage account. They were so tiny. The bartender could barely see their little heads over the counter, but they all knew who they were.

The kids went to a local private school by the name of "All Star Academy." Just to put it all into context; I would show up to school in the morning following other cars in the drop-off line as I drove behind, limousines, Bentleys, and a lot of very expensive cars.

Boca is like a small utopia with people who all had to be better than the next person, having more expensive cars, bigger houses and so on. I couldn't stand snobs and still am the same way today. Life isn't about what you own. If there was a Honda in that line-up, it was surely the nanny dropping off the kids.

Even though we had money, I still wore my jean shorts, tank tops, and flip flops. I never had a cleaning lady, cooked homemade meals, and was very involved in my children's lives raising them alone and juggling everything to make sure all was in order.

Teaching figure skating, power skating for minor hockey, working with the Florida Panthers, running a factory, and raising two children required enormous organizational skills. It was the only way to survive without everything becoming chaotic and out of control. I had no choice but to be efficient to survive. *People called me Superwoman. I have always been the "go to" person.*

The children had a lot of fun in their younger years enjoying playing outside. School always went well. My daughter would jump on her four-wheeler and zoom around the neighborhood to visit her friends. My son used to play on the swing set outside and loved swimming in the pool. We used to have a lot of get-togethers and parties with our friends and neighbors. There was always something to celebrate.

The holidays were wonderful. Easter was so funny. I would put baby powder on a stuffed animal and make paw prints outside on the walkway. Easter morning would come around and the kids would run to the front door. One year they opened the door and found the paws prints. My daughter hollered and ran to the garage, jumped up as usual, hit the garage door opener, pulled on her helmet, and chased after the paws prints thinking she would catch the Easter bunny. *I still laugh at that memory.*

Christmas was similar. They would fight fatigue trying to stay awake and put their sleeping bags next to the Christmas tree thinking they would catch Santa Claus. Every year I put up a massive 12-foot tree filled with gifts that had no end. Now, I dread the holidays after my spirit was taken away from me. After 2000 life had no more meaning. It was all about survival.

## Married Life Begins

ONE DAY WE decided to meet our friends in New York, so our extended family came to Florida to watch the children. My ex and I got on a plane and flew to New York to meet our friends from Connecticut (*the couple we met on our honeymoon*). We had a great time visiting the city and eating in great restaurants. We even chartered a private sailboat that sailed toward the Statue of Liberty. I remember it being overcast that day and quite choppy. I got so nauseous I wanted to throw up.

On our way back to Florida I surprised our family friends from Montreal with tickets to an Eagles concert. It was our gift for having babysat the children while we were in New York.

We drove down to Miami to see the Eagles that day and as I sat down in our seats, my ex walked away and came back two minutes later with a joint in his hand and said, "Look what someone gave me."

Little did I know he probably didn't get it from anyone and already had it in his pocket.

There were a bunch of signs that I never detected back in those days. He used to hide and keep secrets about everything. I never had a peaceful day, always wondering what was going on in his mind and what he was doing. He was a compulsive liar and used to go around hiding things in his pockets.

He was excellent at hiding his secret life, and even me, I was unable to detect anything, but I knew something was wrong.

Family used to come back-and-forth to visit us given we lived in Florida. Our friends from Connecticut came down with the children and we went up to Disney for a weekend and had the time of our lives. We had a lot of good times outside of the hidden life he was living.

*Being in Barbados, and enjoying the weather, the ocean has given me a very calm spirit to be able to write this book. There are many reasons that I decided to do this.*

*First and foremost, was to create therapy for myself.*

*Secondly, I wish to raise awareness for other women that are going through similar things I went through and don't have the strength to get through it.*

*Thirdly, to bring out the truth so that my family, his family, and my children know exactly what happened.*

We started to look for a business. The Woodfield Country Club had a strip mall that was being built outside the front gates, surrounded by an elementary school, a middle school, and a high school.

After doing some market research, we decided to look at the potential to open a popcorn store.

Shortly after, our friends and neighbors in Woodfield introduced us to an Italian family who were looking to sell half of their business as the parents wanted to retire. We spent three months working inside the business learning how to make fresh pasta and understanding the dynamics of a food factory. The products were of high quality, and the receivables were running very well. They had clients such as the Breakers Hotel in Palm Beach, Disney, Carnival cruise lines, and Carnival airlines, along with the majority of local restaurants and Country Clubs.

We saw the potential in this business and decided to give it a go. On the onset we invested half a million dollars to buy 50% shares of the company.

We had 32 Mexican employees working under our guidance. Half the factory was machine operated and the other half was handmade products of high-end quality. I enjoyed working there and learning more and more every day. The Mexican women were very hard-working and very loyal to us.

Every day I went to the store and bought some chicken or meat in order to make a filling for the homemade tacos that our employees made for us, fresh every morning. In return, I gave them bags of the second cut pasta for them to take home to their

## Married Life Begins

families. These were our uneven cuts that would accumulate at the end of every batch. We couldn't package them because they weren't perfectly sized, but they were delicious, nonetheless.

They were grateful for this every day given they were very poor and didn't have the means to eat anything but their native food. The loyalty went too far one day when Ermelinda came into work, and I saw a look of sadness on her face. I asked her what was wrong. She shared with me that she woke up that morning and found her 13-year-old son Jesus dead in his bed.

I freaked out and couldn't believe that she was standing at work after such a horrible tragedy. I grabbed her, put her in my car, drove her back home to the farms, and helped them in any way that I could.

Her son had suffered from heart disease from the onset of his birth, and that day was the end of his life. This woman was so loyal and dedicated to us and dedicated to her family to earn money to be able to put food on the table hence the reason she came in to work that day.

I gave her two weeks off and told her to tend to the funeral and family matters, and that she was going to be paid, regardless. She cried and held me in her arms. To this day I will never forget her.

That same year, I fell pregnant with my third child. I remember how I felt when it happened. I was standing in our walk-in fridge in the pasta factory where I was moving a box from one shelf to the other. I suddenly felt a strange flutter in my stomach. The next day, I started bleeding. I quickly called my gynecologist and went to see her to be told I just had a miscarriage.

Knowing now how life turned out, I cannot even fathom the thought of having had three children to feed with everything that happened.

WHEN I TURNED 30, my mother fell ill and died at the age of 57 after quadruple bypass surgery. Earlier that same year, was her last trip to Florida to visit with us.

We spent years working and as the company grew, we started a second shift at night. Our operations were running 24/7.

We started to do more wholesale distribution having partnered up with Cheney Brothers, sending pasta to New York and all over the United States.

I was working like a dog while my ex sat in his office, pretending to work. I often worked the day shift, went home at dinner to see my babies, then would come back and check on the night shift operations.

Thankfully we had Mr. Bell, our British butler who picked the children up from school, fed them dinner, and watched over them. They loved him and loved eating his mac and cheese.

It came to the point where we needed to do an expansion in the factory and buy more machinery. We went to the bank to get a loan in order to fund the new machinery. This is where the horror of our situation came out. We didn't know this at the time, but our partner was scamming us.

We invested another half-a-million in machinery. When the machinery arrived in South Florida, we discovered that it was missing the entire inside. It had arrived as empty shells!

Soon afterwards our partner told us he wanted to buy us out. We decided to sell our half of the factory because he began to threaten us. He started to pay us in lump sums every month and after the fourth month, the money stopped coming in.

We got lawyers to tend to the problem, but it became very complicated. He started to threaten us and my children if we were to pursue him legally. I found out shortly afterwards that my ex was also stealing money from the company.

THINGS GOT MORE difficult when the money stopped coming in. We put the house on the market after eight years and moved to a beautiful apartment complex that had townhouses. We stayed there for a year then moved into a rental home

## Married Life Begins

until we could figure things out. It was a great home with an in-ground pool and on the same street as our friends.

One day as I was standing in the kitchen ironing, I got a call from one of my neighbors saying there was a bunch of unmarked cars at the local gas station just around the corner.

Next thing I knew those unmarked cars showed up in my driveway and I could see them from my kitchen window. A woman came out of the car and came to the door while a man stood outside in the driveway looking around.

She rang the doorbell, and I went to the door and opened it. She flashed an FBI badge and said, "Hello, my name is ChiChi. I'm with the FBI." My mouth dropped to the floor as I stood there staring at the FBI standing at my front door. What the hell. Was this a joke?

I invited her into the kitchen, and we sat at the table.

She started explaining that we had bought into a company with people who had scammed many families over the years, and that the FBI was following them. She asked, "If you were able to recuperate your money, how much would that be?"

I told her the amount. She went on to tell us that we did nothing wrong and that we were victims just like all the other families. At that point we decided to move back home, so I called the moving company and made the arrangements.

After spending ten years in South Florida, it was time to return.

# The Horror Begins to Unfold

It was August 2000 when we returned home to be near our families and friends. We rented a duplex, temporarily with the plan to look for a home. My ex got a job at our friend's restaurant, and I started to look for a job in figure skating.

In January, after having been in Canada for three months, my ex-husband announced that he was going to South Florida for a long weekend to visit some friends. Upon his return, he entered the house with his suitcase, put it down in the entrance and said hello.

I approached him to say hello and went to take the luggage to start emptying it and doing his laundry. He told me not to touch it and that he was leaving. I asked him where he was going, and he answered, "I'm leaving you."

My son and daughter who were 8 and 10 years old, respectively, at the time were in shock as he left the house. My son went to his room and sat in his bed facing the wall and just stared.

The next morning, I found him sitting in his room, not talking, not responding to me. I tried to talk to him and console him, but he wasn't answering me. He didn't want to eat or do

## The Horror Begins to Unfold

anything. I started to get scared, so I called the pediatrician, and made an appointment immediately.

When I got there, he told me that my son was going through a trauma and advised me to get family counselling as quickly as possible. I called the local family services in our city and explained what happened. They took us right away. We were allowed 10 free sessions with them, which helped us tremendously. However, I couldn't afford to continue private counselling after those 10 sessions.

Given he walked out, emptied out the bank accounts, stole all of our money and left 5-cents in the account, I was in big trouble. All the years I worked teaching competitive figure skating, making a big salary, and the salary from the factory was gone. Because our accounts were joint, he had access to all my savings.

The end of the month was approaching, and I started to panic. I needed to find a way to pay for rent and food. Although I had started to work teaching figure skating at the local ice arena, I certainly wasn't making enough money to pay $900 monthly rent, food, gas, and everything else the children needed.

I called legal aid for help and opened up a file with them. Legal aid isn't like private attorneys, so everything takes a very long time. After eight months of trying to work with them and struggling to make ends meet, legal aid didn't do much for me. My ex did everything possible to not pay child support. I starved, daily, focusing only on the children's needs.

I woke up on Sept 11, 2001, took the children to school and came back home. I jumped into the shower and then sat on the foot of my bed brushing my hair and turned on the television. Every station was showing the 9–11 attack in New York. I remember sitting there in shock and could barely move.

That day, I received an envelope in the mail with our financial investment statements. I hadn't seen them in about nine months because my ex had emptied all the paperwork from our filing cabinet. I had no trace of anything given everything was in his name.

I took the statements to legal aid, and she said, "Oh, now that there is money you will have to start paying me."

I was so furious at her. I called my father and told him what was happening. He instructed me to get my file from her and to wait in the car for his call.

I got to the legal aid office and walked in and asked for my entire file. The legal aid attorney said to me, "You want your file?"

I said, "Yes, give me my file. You are no longer representing me. I will be in the waiting room waiting on you."

My father called me back, gave me the name of his attorney and their address and told me to drive there. The legal aid attorney showed up in the waiting room with my file and said, "Here you go, good luck." I turned to her and answered, "It is you who will need luck."

I got into my car with my legal file and drove out to my father's attorney's office. As I walked in, I asked for the lawyer. They asked me to sit down and wait. A few minutes later she walked out.

Before me stood a tall broad-shouldered woman who shook my hand as tight as can be. I went into her office and sat down and handed her my file. As I quietly sat there, she turned through the pages and shook her head. I just waited and was nervous about how much this was going to cost. I didn't want to burden my father in any way. He was already helping us.

I continued to watch her go through the pages of the file. She turned to me and said, "I'm so sorry you're going through this." She instructed me to go home and take care of the children and that I would get a call from her the next day.

In a panic, I asked her how much this was going to cost me. She reached out and placed her hand on my hand and said, "Go home and take care of the children. I'll get back to you."

I was so nervous and confused and couldn't understand where this was going. There was a trusting look on her face as I got up and left the office and headed home to the children.

## The Horror Begins to Unfold

The next morning around 11 a.m., I received a call from my sister-in-law. She asked, "What did you do? Don't think you're going to go after any money."

I had no idea what she was talking about but the only thing I said was "Fuck you, he has children to support just as I do. He took all my money." and I hung up the phone.

I wondered what on earth had happened because I had no idea why she would've made that call to me. So, I called my attorney and told her what had just happened.

She told me she had gone down to the courthouse at 9 o'clock in the morning under emergency measures and requested a seizure before judgement of all of my ex's personal belongings, his trust fund, and his car.

I couldn't believe it. For months and months, I wondered how I was going to get out of this mess I was in. An angel had come into my life, and this was my attorney who ended up becoming a very good friend. I stayed with her for about 10 years as he dragged me in and out of court. We built a solid file for about a year with back-and-forth incidents that had happened.

From that moment on, I started to log everything that was going on so that I could remember every detail when we went to court for the divorce. There were so many things that happened along the way that had discredited him as a father and as an individual. I knew there was something wrong with him, as he was constantly unstable. I used to say that he's basically digging his own grave. All the decisions and actions he took were taken out of spite, therefore it only harmed him even more.

He would find any way to sabotage the children's activities. He would neglect taking my son to his hockey practices or tournaments if they were on his weekend. The back-and-forth exchanges in a journal, implemented by the court, were toxic and destructive. He found any way to harm the children.

I would receive emails from my son's hockey coach time after time letting me know that my son missed a tournament or a game. In his warped, sick mind, he thought it was a way of harming me by keeping his son home rather than allowing him to play a sport he loved and be with his fellow teammates — many who were his friends.

He showed up at the house one day and started screaming in the streets saying, "Give me my guns!"

Once again, I called the police and they had to intervene. I constantly feared for our lives. There was never a second where I wasn't suffering from anxiety. It was so hard and never ended.

To make things worse, Sept 18, 2001, my father called me around 4 p.m. I assumed he was calling to wish me a happy birthday. He started to explain that he and his wife had gone out to do their errands for the day. When they returned home, they found the fire department at their home. My father was a victim of intentional arson and the entire home along with his dogs and birds he used to breed were gone. The only thing left was the shirt on his back.

We lost everything. I dashed to my father to find him in a state of shock sitting in a metal chair staring at the immense hole in the ground with nothing left of his life's work and family belongings. We lost every photo album, memories, family movie reels, etc.

My father and his wife, of course, came to live with us. This was a time I will always cherish. We were together during the most difficult tragedies imaginable.

My son had bunk beds, so I moved my daughter into his room and my father and his wife moved into my daughter's room.

This went on for about 11 months as I watched my father lose sleep and try to detail every single belonging he could remember to submit to the insurance company. The insurance company, of course, gave him a hard time and my father had to fight for everything. His stress level was through the roof, but he always tended to the children, which I am certain was his reason for living. Unfortunately, one day while in the arena watching my son's hockey game, he stepped outside to get some air and the staff in the rink, who knew me very well because I coached figure skating, came running in screaming that my father had collapsed outside.

## The Horror Begins to Unfold

With the ambulance on its way, I ran to my father's side to find he had had a stroke which then was followed by an aneurysm Then, he suffered a second aneurysm at the hospital with no hope or way to save him.

I was devastated. We had to go get my grandmother and tell her that her eldest of six children had hours to live.

With everything that was going on, my life had taken a serious turn for the worse as I now had to bury my father.

I felt so alone, terrified, and hurt. The pain was unbearable, and I didn't know how to go on. I just wanted to die. My children were all I could see and live for.

I was a zombie just trying to get through every day with the only focus, once again, my children. They too were suffering, having lost their grandfather who they loved very much.

How could life get any worse? I couldn't bear life anymore and felt as though I would suffer forever.

Well, it just didn't let up. I had no strength, no hope. As I write this, it all comes back and I feel a horrible pain so deep, I can't even begin to explain. The courts forced visitation. It seems as though the disasters my ex was causing weren't enough and the children weren't safe. I had to keep fighting and fighting, but justice takes an eternity. The children would call every time and repeatedly tell me they were hungry, their father was always in the bathroom and that it smelled like a skunk.

My anxiety was at the highest level possible. I could barely breathe.

One day my son asked him to take him home early because he wanted to be with me and felt uncomfortable with his father. He got angry and without telling me a word, he drove him home, told him to get out of the car, popped open his trunk and made my son lift his big hockey bag along with his school backpack and left him alone in the street in front of the house. He was nine years old, and I wasn't even home! When I returned home with my daughter, I found my son sitting outside in the dark, alone, scared, and waiting for me to arrive.

This sick bastard did everything possible to harm these children as I had to juggle the constant abuse and bullshit. There was something wrong with his mind and no one in his family understood how he could be so destructive using hatred and anger to punish his family.

He wasn't normal. Clearly, he suffered from depression, and bad behavior and judgement. He showed a lack of maturity and social skills which reached its peak around the age of 28 where from then on, life became a nightmare on a daily basis.

On the other side, there was my daughter who was a competitive elite figure skater. She too suffered from her father's abuse as he would cause her enormous stress by telling her he wasn't going to take her to her training sessions or her competitions when it was his weekend with the kids. She would let him know in advance of her schedule and he would menace her by telling her it was his weekend, and he would do as he pleased.

Because she refused his way of harming her, she stood up to him and refused to go with him on the weekends she had important events. She was strong and brave and clearly knew right from wrong.

He had visitation every Wednesday night and every second weekend. One Wednesday night he picked up the children from school and was supposed to take them for dinner and to the library to do their homework. Instead, he took them to an outdoor park in the winter, put my son's skates on him and had him stand in the goalie net with no equipment or protective gear while he shot pucks at him.

Early in the evening I got a call from him, asking me for my son's Medicare card. I started to feel a sense of panic and asked him what was going on. He told me there was an accident and I needed to take him to the clinic.

I asked him where they were and rushed over to that clinic to find my son sitting in the backseat of his car, with a huge welt on his forehead and barely responding to me. I was enraged and out of control in my mind. I told my ex to get the hell out of there. I grabbed my son, put him in my car and rushed down to the

## The Horror Begins to Unfold

Montreal Children's Hospital. I double parked and ran into the hospital with him in my arms. I went straight to the wicket to ask for help. I hollered, "Please help me. Please help me. My son is in trouble." The nurse got up from her chair and looked over the window ledge and saw my son sitting on the bench barely responding.

The next thing I knew a team of doctors were running out, grabbed him from my arms and took him into the back to the emergency room. They asked me to sit down and be patient. I was shaking and terrified. This never would have happened had he not been with him. About 20 minutes later the doctor came out and said, "What on earth happened here? Why did this happen?" I asked him what was wrong with my son. He told me my son had suffered a skull fracture and sounded furious when he asked me how on earth that happened. After overnight care they sent us home the following day with a sheet of instructions on how to deal with a massive concussion.

Child services came to our home to check on the children. When something like this happens, it's normal they will wonder if the child was abused. After visiting our home on several occasions, they understood that the children were in a loving home and were safe.

The children continued to go with him for visitation and each time, there was some kind of drama that occurred. I can't begin to describe the daily anxiety, lack of sleep I suffered, and heart palpitations every single day as I looked over my shoulders and had to find ways to battle the constant daily dramas he caused.

School work was never completed. Projects weren't done on his time. The school called me often to tell me the children were anxious. Every day was turmoil.

Shortly afterwards, the children went to his house for the weekend. He was supposed to bring them back on a Sunday. My son was at his hockey Christmas party. One of the parents from the hockey party brought my son back home to me but my daughter was still at his house.

I called him to ask him when he was going to bring her home. In response, he yelled and screamed and swore at me. He told me I would never see her again.

I called him back and told him this wasn't going to go well for him and that I would come and pick her up. He told me to go *!#! myself and slammed the phone. I called the police in a panic. They instructed me to show up and wait outside his house until they got there. Several police cars arrived and a supervisor van as well. They got out of the car as one of the police officers walked over to me and instructed me to stay in the car. I was shaking beyond imagination.

I watched them walk up to his front door and knock. I saw them knock again. The door opened just a slight bit and I watched the officer push the door and grab him by his shirt and pin him up against the wall. Minutes later, my daughter came running out of the house in her socks, holding her clothes and her boots in her hands while she ran through the snow yelling, "Mommy, Mommy!" I jumped out of the car and grabbed her in my arms. She asked me to never make her go there again. I consoled her in my arms and told her she will always stay with Mommy.

The police came to my car and let me know that they were going to write up a report and advised me to call a lawyer and do something about what just happened. He told me that my ex was unstable. I called my lawyer the next morning and told her what had happened and also sent her the police report. I then said, "I don't care what the courts ordered. I don't care what the law is, my children aren't leaving my home again to go anywhere with him."

My attorney took the police report of that incident to the courts and that's when the visitation immediately stopped. A court ordered psychosocial expert was appointed to our case. They met with me alone, with him alone, with me and the children, and with him and the children.

They determined that he wasn't fit to take the children and removed his visitation and told him to get help. He continued

# The Horror Begins to Unfold

to stalk us for years. I was terrified everyday living in hiding, as much as I could. The children grew and I constantly watched over every single thing.

My daughter got a job at the local mall. He would follow her and would videotape her when she was working at the shopping center in a shoe store. He would show up at the bank where I worked and cause problems. That one time when he showed up at the bank, I got out of my seat, went back into the staff kitchen, and told my boss I was going to wait there until he left the building. He called the ombudsman's office and made a complaint against me when I wasn't even anywhere near him. This caused me a little bit of trouble, but as I explained the situation to my boss, they understood. I was terrified of losing my job which meant "no food".

He went again to my daughter's workplace and videotaped her working inside of the store. One day she called me crying and saying, "Mommy what's wrong with him? Why is he doing this? Please make this stop."

Once again, I called the police and filed a complaint against him. The police officer came to my place of work. I sat down with her and wrote the police report. After finishing our complaint, she left and told me she would be in touch with me soon. I then discovered she had gone to his residence and arrested him. He spent the night in jail and was released the next day, because I decided not to press charges. But instead, I warned him that if he were to come near her again that I would call the police and have him arrested again. He was completely out of control and was clearly on a mission to destroy me and the children. He was filled with hatred and anger and only wanted to harm us in any way that he could.

After 10 years, I was so tired and fed up with struggling and having to deal with him. He tried to get full custody of the children and dragged me into court for years where he would ask for the children's beds and thought he would get custody of them.

In awe, the judge had asked him where the children would sleep at my house if he were to take their beds. His entire goal was to find a way to stop paying child support so he could have more money to finance his delinquent way of life. He never, ever considered or cared for his children or their welfare and quality of life.

It became unbearable and I didn't know how else to make it stop. I just prayed every day that he would go away. I spent years and years looking over my shoulder, wondering if he was following us, wondering if he was going to stalk the children, and not knowing how to get out of the situation.

IN 2009, I met a young man who was 28 years old at the time who suffered from severe drug addiction. It was so bad that it destroyed his life and his family. We connected and he trusted me. I asked him if he would write a book with me on his life to help others. So, he did.

He admitted himself into rehab and I spent the following year or so going to the rehab center almost every weekend and writing the story of his life with him. When I asked him if he would write his story with me, I saw another side of him; a side that felt validated. He wanted to tell his story and make a difference. He felt important and every time I arrived at the center, he was excited to see me and write the book.

All the other patients now looked up to him and encouraged him with regards to this project. His self-esteem had shifted towards the positive. He felt cool amongst the other patients he lived with. He walked around with his head held high. At Christmas of that year, my children and I baked cookies and brought them to the families at the rehab center. I always taught my children that Christmas was for giving. In fact, I always believed in giving to others.

His mother became my best friend and is still my confidante and the person who has always been by my side. My career at the bank helped me get to where I am today. I had to constantly advance through many jobs to keep building better financial stability for me and my children.

In 2010 I published the book both in English and French. I did a book launch at Chapters and donated all of the proceeds to the local community shares organization that helps underprivileged families. Soon after I launched the book, I got a call from Brenda Herzog, the drug rehab placement specialist that gave me a testimonial which was written on the back of my book. She told me she had received a call from a man who was talking about the book. She asked him, "Sir, what book are you talking about?" He answered that it was his ex-wife's book and told her my name. He asked her for help and asked if it was too late for him to go to rehab after so many years of using drugs. She told him it was never too late for someone who wanted to get clean.

> "The first time I spoke with Ally, I felt an instant connection. The pureness of her heart shone through her words as she spoke of seeking help for her friend. As a Rehab Placement Specialist, I knew immediately that Ally possessed what it takes to help, not by enabling, but by being there and offering love and support, which is what every addict needs. She had her boundaries set, and the strength to stand by them. In a perfect world everyone with a loved one suffering addiction would have the knowledge and understanding that exudes from Ally's soul.
>
> I am going to be promoting this book, A Testimonial of Insanity, to every rehabilitation centre I have in my database. I do this with respect and my belief that this book will touch the lives of everyone that has the privilege of reading it.
>
> Thank you Ally, it is a blessing to have such a gifted author's work out there for everyone to read."
>
> Brenda Herzog
> Addiction Rehab Placement Specialist

He went to one of the most successful rehab centers in Canada where he spent eight weeks there and $28,000 later to try and stop taking drugs. His drug of choice was marijuana. YES, marijuana: morning, noon, and night.

I received a call from the center asking me if we would like to participate in family therapy. She stated that the rehab program included family therapy and offered this to us free of charge.
I told her we lived in Montreal and that it was much too far and that we had already dealt with therapy on our own. I thanked her for her time and hung up the phone.

About three months later I received an email from him that sounded like it was dictated. It stated something to the effect of "Thanks for taking care of the children when I couldn't."

An addict must write his confessions and apologize as part of his treatment.

After everything he had done to me, there was no room for forgiveness. The trust had been broken, and there was no way I was going to get myself back into a situation that took me over 10 terrible years to get out of. He was a devil. He had no heart and no compassion for his children whatsoever. He was vindictive and evil, and only wanted to harm us.

I continued to promote the book as it started circulating in rehab centers.

Trouble from him became a norm in my life. I never felt safe or relaxed since the day we met. Today, I suffer from anxiety pretty much all the time.

I received a letter in the mail from yet another lawyer. He had gone through so many lawyers, I lost count. I called this clown and asked him what the hell he wanted. He started to go on about how my ex has no money and that he cannot pay child support. I told him I wanted to meet with him and gave him an appointment to meet me next to my place of work. I left during my lunch hour to go next door to a cafe to meet this lawyer. He started with his pity story about my ex having no money.

I raised my voice and said, "He has no money?" I lost it and told him it was me who has had no money for the last 12 years after having my bank account emptied, raising two children alone, working three jobs to make ends meet. I asked him if he knew who my ex was; if he knew who the family was, and that he was the heir to a fortune left by his father who owned one of the biggest engineering firms in the world.

I told him that he walked out on a family and spent the last 12 years tormenting us. I told him that he was a drug addict, harmed me and his children, and has had me in and out of court for over 10 years, depleting every cent I tried to earn to keep fighting for my children. I told him how food was scarce. I told this lawyer to shut his mouth when he had no idea about the truth.

He went silent and had nothing to say. I told him to draw up the papers and to stop child support. I wanted my ex to get the hell away from us and preferred to work harder than to ever have to deal with him ever again. That day was the end of any contact or abuse I would ever have to deal with again.

I took on job after job, working in day care, serving at a friend's restaurant part time on weekends, cleaning office buildings at midnight, and begging for work so I could try and support my children. The heaviness of the financial and emotional trauma was impossible to endure.

ALTHOUGH, AFTER THAT there should have been silence, but he was still lurking around. I could feel his presence and often would see a car sitting in the streets with its lights on parked not too far. I didn't know what kind of car he drove but somehow I knew in my heart it was him.

# THE DOWNWARD SPIRAL BEGINS

Years went by again, and when my son was about 20 years old, I found out that he had reconnected with his father. This terrified me and when I confronted him, he told me not to worry. Of course, I was worried because I feared he may be negatively influenced, start lying, and hiding things about his life.

Guess what happened?

I used to go into his room to collect his dirty clothes from his laundry basket as well as his gym bag. One day while I stepped into his room, I suddenly stopped in my tracks as I noticed something unreal. For a moment, I thought I was dreaming.

"How could this be? Please God, no!"

He was lying to me about everything that was going on in his life, things I cannot write. I wanted to die. My baby was going in the direction that I spent his whole life teaching him was wrong. I felt as though I was reliving another horror like the one I had just started to recover from. How much more could I bear? Why was this happening? I couldn't for the life of me understand why.

Yes, I spoiled my children. Yes, I was that mother who did everything for them, therefore getting entitlement in return. My own fault. But who is to say that had I not done too much for them that things would have turned out differently.

Today, it seems that the majority of that generation feels entitled. I hear it often from other parents my age. In our day, we never spoke back to our parents or disrespected them. We didn't dare. It would have been disgraceful. Today, there are no limits.

I confronted him when he got home and the familiar lies had just begun, the same lies I lived through with his father.

I told him there was no way I was going to tolerate his behavior. I began to see my life falling apart right before my eyes. There is only so much one human can take.

I told him to leave the house, that I wasn't going to live through this again. It was too painful having to deal with his father, and now my son?! No way! He had to leave. I saw quickly that he was brainwashed and knew I had no power to change his mind.

I noticed that he had the same addictive personality his father had. I guess it was possible to have carried the addictive gene.

I prayed every day for God to help me, to help him, to shine a light of hope. I couldn't sleep as it was; and now I really couldn't sleep.

He left the house for four months and one day he came to see me to talk. He had been staying with a friend; so I thought. He told me he wanted to come home.

I accepted, but spent every day in agony, checking what was going on. Looking for clues became a daily ritual.

I APPLIED FOR a position internally at the bank I was working for and finally moved into a management position in a downtown branch.

I started there in March of 2012. I had a great team and was able to use my talents in customer service and superior sales to train my team and always surpass our monthly objectives in sales.

I bought a house in 2012, which I never thought I would ever be able to do on my own. The children and I were all on the mortgage. There was no other way to accomplish this and purchase a home. Five years later, I was able to renew my mortgage and remove them from the loan in order to liberate them. I worked so hard so that they could be free of this responsibility. I did it!

It is my custom, renovated, and charming home that I love dearly. I put my heart and soul into my home to make it a magnificent place to live. I renovated the entire house and finally put everything the way I wanted without any compromise, just exactly what I wanted.

But then something horrible happened. After four months of renovating, I came home one day,and tried to open the front door but found it was hard to open. When I got into the house, the walls and ceilings were full of open cracks everywhere.
I couldn't believe my eyes.

I ran to my neighbor's house and asked her to come over and see what was going on. She is a project manager and deals with renovation projects. She panicked and started making calls.
A structural engineer and a soil engineer came to the house to assess the situation. I was told that there was structural damage that wasn't disclosed to me. Given it was all underground, we couldn't see any of it when we inspected the house. My beautiful, newly renovated house was sinking on one side, like the Leaning Tower of Piza.

I had to come up with over 50K just to fix the foundation. To fix it they had to demolish all the walkways, the backyard deck, which we just renovated, and all the grass.

I was terrified and didn't know how I would find the money. I called my lawyer, and she started a file against the prior owner. One day I was in bed and my daughter woke me up to tell me the house was moving. I jumped out of bed, grabbed both children, and both dogs and we ran outside. We stood in the street staring at the house as my heart was palpitating. My daughter had her cell phone with her. She looked at her phone

# The Downward Spiral Begins

and said, "Mom, we just had an earthquake." So, I went online on the phone and yes, it was an earthquake. I was so relieved. It was only an earthquake!

Finding the money was another huge obstacle. I couldn't afford this. I went to my bank and was able to get a line of credit for 35k. It wasn't enough. Suddenly, my friend offered to lend me the rest until we could take the former owner to court. Three years went by as it took forever to settle in court all while having to pay for a mortgage and pay the line of credit. I was financially depleted and endured yet another series of second and third jobs to try and get by. I fought to get through this disaster.

After they repaired the foundation, I now had to have the front steps, walkways, deck and all the grass redone. It was overwhelming. I was terrified I would lose my home. Job after job, chipping away to just barely make it every month.

We went to court, and I won my case. The judge was disgusted at what the former owner had done and not only decided to award the amount we requested, but even more.

I thought I would be out of the woods, until about a week later, when my lawyer received a letter stating the former owner had filed for bankruptcy and I had no hope of collecting any money from her. The debt had now reached 100k after all the work, engineer fees, legal fees, court fees and the rebuilding of the exterior.

I refinanced the house and found myself with an even bigger mortgage. Years went by as I struggled to carry all this financial strain, but it worked out, somehow, given I never stopped working 2–3 jobs at a time. I was so exhausted every day, balancing my day-to-day responsibilities.

Eventually after years of pushing and working hard, my financial life got a little bit easier, and I was proud to finally be able to carry a mortgage on my own. Although money was tight, we found a way to manage. The children gave me a small amount of money to pay for their cell phone bills every month.

We managed all together as we always did since the day my ex left. I could depend on the kids as they could obviously depend on me to carry all the responsibilities. Their presence alone gave me a reason to go on. They needed me and I needed them. I couldn't sleep until both of them were safe at home any time they were out and about.

Everything I did, I did for them. I never put myself first.

My daughter worked hard in life, saving as much money as she could. She worked hard and excelled at every job even though she never continued school into university. Having no degree, her options were limited, so she stayed in sales, and she was good at it.

My son, the scholar, could have spent his life in school. He never had enough of studying and prefers to be behind the scenes instead of on the front line.

He studied mechanical engineering technology, graduated, went to his first job, and then quit after one day. Then, he wanted to be a general contractor but decided to get his carpentry license first. He again graduated but then decided he didn't want to do carpentry.

I was dizzy. He sat in his room day in and day out, living as an introvert. It was like pulling teeth to get him to do anything. Every day was a battle. Every day he sat there as I watched his life go by with no goals, no saving money, nothing at all.

His presence and behavior worried me constantly and I started to lose hope.

He would work at a friend's restaurant as a server, with one degree after another, just sitting there doing nothing but restaurant work, playing video games until 4 a.m., waking us up, being irresponsible, getting parking tickets, and not taking responsibility for his life. He was oblivious to everything around him and concentrated on his introverted life.

It is amazing how no matter what we do to guide our children, at some point they must be accountable for their own life, and I couldn't influence him no matter what and how I did it.

My kids wondered why I was so stressed and why I never had hope. They don't understand at all. It takes a wise and intuitive person to get it.

# The Downward Spiral Begins

I cannot even describe the anxiety I was living with. My children are my life and always were. No one can understand this feeling I had but me. Everyone's experiences are different and only I understand what I went through.

I thought the children were fine after we went through therapy. People said my son was just a quiet boy. I couldn't possibly be inside his head to understand everything. From the outside both my children seemed just fine, but I suppose anybody who goes through what we went through will surely be affected. It's almost impossible not to. No matter how good the parents or the surroundings are, we cannot control everyone. The best we can do is instill good morals, values, and family unity, and pray it all works out.

My son resented me for years, blaming me for not having seen his father. I tried to explain, as best as I could, but I could see in his eyes that he was negatively influenced. There was nothing to do. He wanted so much to have his father in his life, that he would have accepted anything about him whether it was right or wrong.

ALL OF THIS that I write is completely normal given the circumstances. I am no different than anyone else who experienced similar situations. The difference is today, I can say, I made it, with the love and support of my family and friends and the strength that I had.

The relationship between me and my son was delicate, and I am the one who resents the fact that he didn't understand things as an adult, but I love him regardless. He is my son, and I am his mother.

LIFE CONTINUED. I eventually left the banking world and started working as a financial manager for a car brand. After I went through the interview process, I got a call and was hired. I was excited about the news and came home to announce it to my children.

"Guys guess what? I got the job." My son mumbled, "Dad works there."

I went silent, then said, "What did you just say?" He repeated the same thing.

I almost fell to the floor. Instead, I screamed. "Of all the damn companies, we had to end up working for the same one?! What the hell!?" I was so angry. Is there just an evil eye hanging over my head? Can I have any more bad luck? When will this end?

The next day I asked to speak to my boss. I explained the situation in a nutshell and basically only stated that it was a difficult divorce and that I preferred not to see him.

He assured me that I would never cross his path because he worked in the building next door and would never have to come to our building. Although I was reassured, I still looked over my shoulder every day.

Our company cafeteria is located in the building across the street where he works. For three years, I never stepped foot in there to get lunch. Apparently, the chef cooks very healthy meals and for a fraction of the price. It is really a great place to eat but I did everything to avoid him.

Each year, when our company's annual Christmas party came around, I would ask my boss if he was going. He would get back to me to inform me that he had confirmed his presence, therefore I would decline my invitation. I felt it was his right to have this time given that his friends at work were a big part of his daily happiness.

I would find a valid excuse when my colleagues would ask why I wasn't going.

## The Downward Spiral Begins

The funniest part of all of this is, my daughter also took on a position occupying the same role as I did but in a sister dealership, but she has just recently left our company to work with her fiancé.

My son had started studying digital marketing, yet another direction that took him years to develop. I felt hopeless as I felt as though he was much too comfortable in mom's house and did nothing to advance himself financially.

It was frustrating to see him sit in his room as years passed and I had to continue to support him and keep a roof over his head. I lost faith as he constantly spoke impolitely and treated me with disrespect instead of taking the role of an adult son knowing the enormous abnormal struggles and sacrifices I made. I was constantly exhausted and today my body suffers.

It's one thing to need to live at home because you need to save enough money to be able to move out on your own but it's another thing to sit there and be a burden, not recognizing your mother scraping to get by and offer of yourself if not monetarily than emotionally and physically just to help in any way.

I have never heard the words, "Mom, I got this. Do you need any help?"

No one understands how drained I have become. The older I get the harder it gets. I continued to push myself mentally and physically.

Everyone thinks I am so strong, but what they don't know is, I suffer from great anxiety, constant worry, and financial stress. Although I earn substantial money now, the trauma from starving and having suffered for so many years remains in my mind.

I move at a million miles a minute to stay in control of everything so that life doesn't pile up and drown me. This is the only way I have ever been able to survive.

After three years of working for the same company, we in fact, never crossed paths. For the first time since 2019, I actually attended our company Christmas party. For the first time in 22 years, I don't look over my shoulder. For the first time since 1988, I am beginning to breathe.

Of course, I harbor a lot of resentment and anger that I must deal with because of the truth that was now a reality and no longer a wonder or suspicion. It is confirmed. It was written and now everything made sense.

I spent months having nightmares, and still do, but less often. I felt disgusted and felt as though I was living inside a movie that would never end.

A certain anxiety immediately came to life. I couldn't believe what I was reading. I couldn't believe that after all these years I was a victim of abuse by the man I married. It is all disgusting and unforgivable. The wounds were cut deeper and everything I started to heal from after 2011 just reopened again like a curse.

How do I get through this? How do I move on when I thought I had moved on? All it was, was a pause button on the remote control of the movie that was my life. How do I accept what has happened? How can I ever trust anyone again?

I can't!

# THE TRUTH REVEALED

He damaged me and created a life of difficulty that became the norm and my daily patterns. I didn't even know how to change it. There is only one thing that will fix and erase the past. The only thing that will give me air to breathe again is for my children to open their eyes and give me the honor and love and validation for what I did. No human can just push through life with such weight and never be taken care of by those they suffered for. I need this to break the 30-year cycle and be given the chance to spend what's left of my life in peace. I continue to pray for this.

I suppose my ex never destroyed his journal knowing that one day I would read it. Twenty-two years after the divorce and his death, only now I find out the truth through his journal.

Well, here it is. The raw truth. Eighty-five pages of which I have pulled only parts of it for this book.

> *I feel as though he chose this to write his rehab journal because of the look of its cover, as well as its colors of green, which may represent Marijuana and the amorphous design of this composition book. This must have attracted him.*

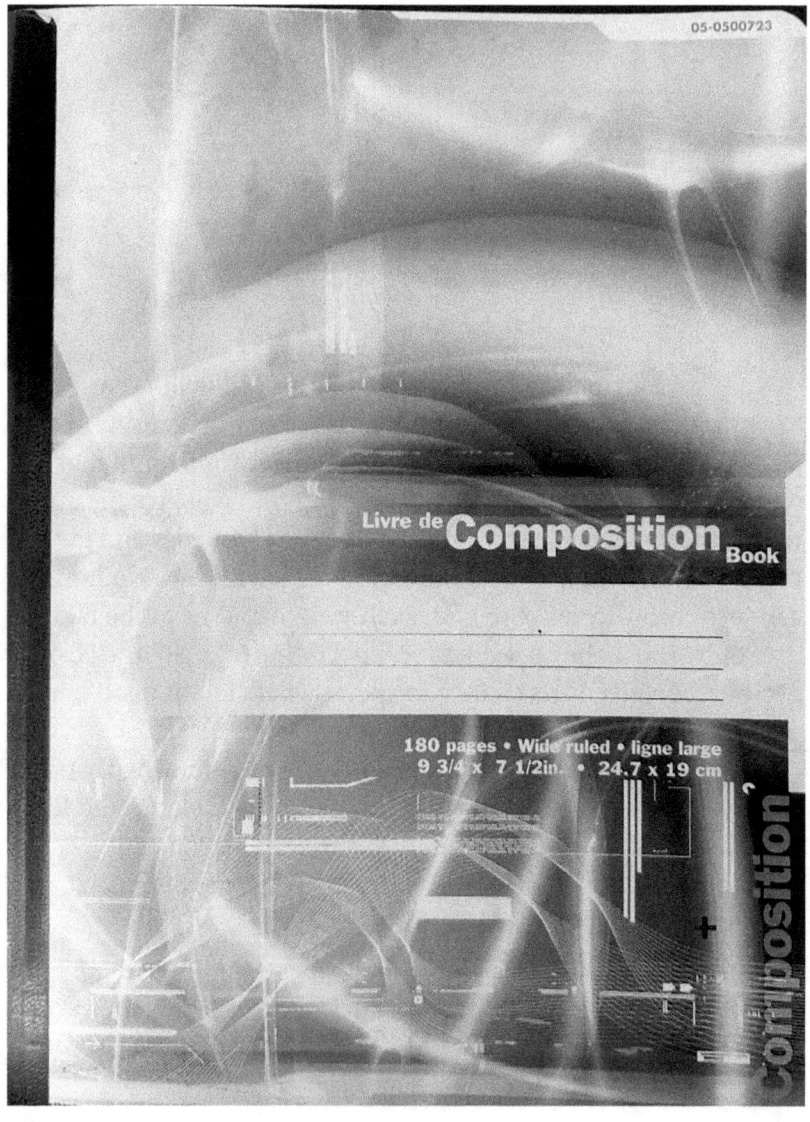

*May 1, 2011, marked his first day in rehab. He describes how he feels scared but anxious to start his therapy because he knows that he chose to do this so he can get better. He says that "mari" (marijuana) creates untrue feelings and unexpected goals. His skin flared up after taking his first niacin pill but on the second day the niacin pill didn't bother him.*

②

3RD. FRI. MAY. 13         SUNNY 20°

Today did not eat breakfast until 11:30. Because of Blood work this morning + URINE + EKG. $UNCH, ½ SANDWICH. TUNA, SAUNA 2 HRS. NIACIN INCREASED. had a first meeting with my conselor, anna felt really good to get rid of emotions and feelings off my chest. mood was good except, for this morning cause no Breaky.

4TH SAT. MAY 14TH    RAIN. 15°

SLEPT. MAYBE 3 HRS head-ach, stomach aches. 5:30 AM WALK outside in the back for an hour. went back to bed for an hour felt sick until I got in the sauna, and had a drink that terry gave me that soothed my stomach. It was a little tough in the sauna for a full day. Still thinking about Alice, and the kids. I would right some more but very tired. So Good night.

5TH SUN. — GOOD DAY AT SAUNA — THOUGHT CLEARING UP

*He talks about how they took blood tests and an EKG to determine the state of health he was in and how to proceed with treatments. He was basically going through what all drug addicts go through, detoxing and adjusting to abstinence. He has been on drugs for 37 years so clearly, he didn't know any other way of life.*

6th. Mon Good day at sauna pain-muscle in neck pretty much gone. Good dinner - Good day in general. Positive Thinking.

7th Got 8 hrs sleep last night. Started the day very well with a positive attitude good day at the sauna and at the gym. good dinner watch the hockey game with the boys. Bill gave me an assignment and when I started reading it I was disapointed as I thought of my x-wife and kids and not a sign of them, no message of encouragement, seems that there is no hope as I reflect on what has happen. I feel like when I get home, pack my bags and go far away.

MAY. 18 – July 5th
wish I could have written all of the emotions and shit that came in and out of my head. But I have worked very hard at this program of 8 weeks and have got all the tools to make my new life a success thanks to Turning Point!

## The Truth Revealed

*He actually expected us to show a sign of encouragement after everything he had done to harm us. Going to rehab doesn't pardon everything in the snap of a finger. Rehab was his therapy—not ours. Forgiveness requires endless efforts of going above and beyond to try and ask for forgiveness and undo all of the terrors that were done, especially toward children.*

(4)

July 5th, 2011  28° sunny

7:00 had three cups of coffee, 7:50 Butch woke up
8:00 ACOPUNTURE meditation, shaved and finished packing
as it was my final day at Turning Point.
did one hour at the sauna and took my
I.Q. Test III, read my plan to work on when
I went home to stay focused on that plan
and daily shedual, picked my stone (Beleive)
read my wish card from John, Tammy, Sascha
with frogs in my throat and tears coming
down my face. I said to myself I love
them we hug and said, see you soon,
Take care and thank-you for giving me
my life back. XXXOOO. J.Y.
I arrived home at around 6:00 PM, picked up
my mail on the floor and quickly went
through my e-mails, I was a little intimidated
then I got some groceries, and positive
talk myself to, use the tools I was tought
I went to bed and told that little voice
to shut-up.

## The Truth Revealed

*It was now his last day in rehab after eight weeks. Got the work pages he needed to work on, in order to stay on track. He hugged everyone, with a lump in his throat and a tear in his eyes.*

(5)

July 6th, 2011 WEDNESDAY    NA 5550 PARK AVENUE - 3D

7:11 AM woke up and said THANK-you, it's going to be a great day! had my coffee and meditation at 8:00 till 8:25, got dressed and ran some aarons, BANK, LEASING OFFICE, came back to get my (Parking spot.) went through some mail, got my phone in order, Bell, wrote a letter of appology to Banque National, did laundry, washed floors, and cleaned bathroom. took a shower, went to listers smoke meat, and orange pop. → went to first N.A. meeting, it was good and met some good people. Great day. Tomorrow will be better.

11:AM SHAKE

(Harassed me when I worked at the bank)

July 7th, 2011  THURSDAY.

7:30 AM WAKE, Thank-you it's a great day! coffee meditation, made a few phone calls on my to do list, went to Ste-Adele, work out 2 hours, had some croissant ham and cheese, lots of water, made a little fire to keep bugs away, bank deposit, got back home mail June payment for bills. ate 2 bananas, took a nap, made steak and salad, tidied up the appartment, cut pineapple for tomorrow, organized papers. took shower, listen to some music.

*He talks about how he sent a letter to the bank I worked at to apologize for what he did.*

> I remember being afraid to lose my job because of the things he invented and caused me trouble when I worked there. The risk of losing my job because of his lies meant not being able to eat. I already starved a lot so I could feed my children.

July 14th, 2011 Thursday
Woke up 6:30am said (thank-you its going to be a great day) coffee, computer. Then realized I had appointment for gym showed up at 8:15, and the girl at the counter said they booked two people so I will go back tuesday at one came back home, tried to meditate but not successfuly. I was tired. took a nap for 1hr. 10:30 got back on my feet. had an emotion of sadness and loneliness, so I did some laundry. Mail man delivered detox powder noticed the exterior was torn and package had powder on it, opened the bag seal was off container opened powder everywhere, called Kelly she told me to send it back I was agitated and pissed off, went to the postal office, and told them off real of and wasn't happy, went to the automatic teller, it smelt like shit or someone probably farted, just a shitty day, went to an NA meeting, then felt better. Gym before.

July 15th, 2011 Friday
Woke up. 7:30 said (thank-you its going to be a good day) coffee, computer, meditation, went to see Adele for 1½ felt a little negativety. probably cause spoke to mom, and found as she was a little bitter about leaving for two months and not telling her about it took a nap woke up felt better. made chicken + corn, shower, went to a meeting.

## The Truth Revealed

*He talks about how he received his detox powder to find it torn open with powder everywhere and how he needed to order another one. He went to the post office to tell them off.*

(10)

very positive feelings + asked Steven to be my sponsor, to me he is not saying no but to call him, cause he has a few people as sponsees and not doing their step-work properly, but good introduction.

July 16th, 2011 SATURDAY.

Woke up 3:30, Coffee. got some milk and cream at the store, thank-you, it's going to be a great day, meditation 20 min computer, journal, going to go to moms and see her. went to see my mom she was worried cause I didn't tell her where I was in the last two months, got to hug her hard, she had tears when I left. need to see her more often. Then went to see ▬▬, was really glad to hug her and spoke about my rehab. she is really open minded, and spoke to me about ▬▬ that her and ▬▬ don't want her to smoke cigarettes but let her smoke-pot instead, as she went on the balcony and light one up. The smell started to come in the condo as I was saying goodbye, and called ▬▬▬▬ soon after and let her know about NA. went to zellers got a salad spinner, went to do groceries, relaxed a bit, took a shower, dinner steak, fajitas, then went to the meeting early, got everyone some tim-bits, did some service.

## The Truth Revealed

*He explains how he told his sister that he was in rehab and that he was conscious that he needed to see his mother more frequently. He shares about meditation, daily repetitive routines, and how he went to see his family to explain only the basic story of his rehab. According to the journal, they don't know everything. As a mother, I recognize that especially when your child dies, it's important to know the truth at some point. And finally, the secrets and truth have come out for his family and all to know.*

July 17th TUESDAY
woke up, said thank, its going to be a great day
had coffee, computer, sort of had mixed emotion
about loneliness, and Alice, missing her and the
kids, so I was in the appartment and kicked
myself out towards the gym called Steven
and he told me to read chapter 5
(What can I do) did some banking and kind of
gave myself to my higher power and read the
chapter and everything made sense, went to
a meeting, was great.

July 29, WEDNESDAY
Woke-up said thank-you its going to be a great
day. coffee, computer, went to buy a batterie
for A TV. will pick-up THURSDAY. went to the
gym early 2:00 had a protein shake, tred-mill
for about ½ hr. then training with Andy.
it was hard and my quad felt like it ripped
from the lunges. so came home after steam bath and

## The Truth Revealed

*He is in his apartment having mixed feelings and emotions. Says he is missing me and the children. Kicked himself out of there and went to the gym and called his sponsor to get advice on how to cope with those feelings, read a chapter from his 12-step program and claimed it made sense and helped him.*

*I imagine he felt great feelings of guilt for what he had done to us.*

AUG. 2nd, 2011, TUESDAY.

Woke up said thank-you, it's going to be a great day! coffee, computer, meditation, laundry, bank balance, organized papers, bills. sharpened chain saw, relaxed watch Godfather, dinner, shower, getting ready for a meeting. also been calling sponsor Steve every day.

AUG. 3rd, 2011, WEDNESDAY.

Wake-up said thank-you, it's going to be a great day, coffee, computer, smoothy, workout with Andy, came home, lunch, tired so took a nap. woke up. took a shower went to Festa's smoke-meat sandwich, went to a meeting.

AUG. 4th, 2011 Woke up said thank-you it's going to be a great day! coffee, computer, got dressed went to NA meeting in French at 12:00 came back had lunch, went to the bank to pay bills, money not transferred yet. came home, tired took a nap. woke up watch T.V. a bit. shower went to place Victoria bought EMINEM CD'S RECOVERY, RELAPSE. went to meeting came home, computer, music, movie better.

*An addict in recovery establishes a very strict routine in order to follow the same functions in the course of a day to not find themselves bored and over thinking thus creating the possibility of relapse. He didn't eat well and typically had fast food several times a day.*

Aug. 18th, 2011 THURSDAY.

Woke up said thank-you its going to be a great day. coffee computer, smoothy, went to a meeting 12:00, came had promo lunch, tofty lep. reading shower, ate dinner went to a meeting came back, computer T.V., Bed.

Aug. 19th, 2011 FRIDAY.

Woke up said thank-you its going to be a great day, computer, smoothy, started to register and get my application in to Ykmarter. by 4:30 I got accepted. went to a meeting shared that. came home started to print materials for the course.

Aug. 20th, 2011 SATURDAY.

Woke up said thank-you its going to be a great day, coffee, computer, ordered my text books, printed the rest of my material. went a little bit through it. ate, took a shower went to make coffee at Saturday night clean. meeting was good. came back computer a little T.V. Bed. 12:00 am.

## The Truth Revealed

*He applied to take a university course on addiction and got accepted. In the essay we found, he discusses the reasons he feels that his father was coping with severe depression. Although his father was a successful engineer in his grandfather's firm, he knew that he was also taking drugs to cope with his depression and wrote about how his mother would find wrappers of a brown gummy substance in his pockets. In the same essay he also divulges that his family has no knowledge of "something" that will show up later on in another page from the journal.*

Step 1.

1. The disease of addiction means using psychoactive drugs or alcohol to relieve emotional pain or physical pain, guilt, shame, and can manifests itself into compulsive behavior.

2. recently my disease has been active recently with excessive use of internet such as facebook, internet games, and dating sites.

3. When I am obsessed with something like internet dating or island paradise, my thinking follows a pattern of browsing for more dates, or adding more to my island. so I dam spend even more time on the computer.

4. When a thought occurs to me I used to immediately act on it without considering the consequences, as dates were not occurring immediately, I use to call escorts to fulfil my immediate needs. I behave compulsively by spending excessive time on the internet dating site and games.

5. the self centered part of my disease affect my life in a way that I take things personaly, and make assumptions and feel guilty, ashamed, anger and resentment. as for others I avoid them, and push them away, stop communicate and isolate myself. and that I don't need any help I have it all figured out.

# The Truth Revealed

*This next page I will rewrite so the message is clear because his handwriting is difficult to read, as I feel it is an important topic on addiction.*

"The disease of addiction means using psychoactive drugs or alcohol to relieve emotional pain or physical pain, guilt, shame, and can manifest itself into compulsive behavior.

"When I'm obsessed with something like internet dating or Island Paradise, my thinking follows a pattern of browsing for more dates, or adding more to my island so I can spend even more time on the computer.

"When a thought occurred to me, I used to immediately act on it without considering the consequences, as dates weren't occurring immediately, I used to call escorts to fulfil my immediate needs. I behave compulsively by spending excessive time on the internet dating site and games."

(31)

6. My disease has affected me physically being tired, lazy and overweight. Mentally with not being able to focus or pay attention or listen to what other people have to say. Spiritually, not connecting with my higher power or a God of my understanding. Emotionally with sadness, anxiety, self-sabotage. Killed all of these aspects.

7. The specific way my addiction manifest itself recently is with internet dating. Thinking how it could be a quick fix to all my problems. Internet Porn, buying escorts in the past.

8. I have been obsessed with my x-wife, and has gotten in the way of my relationships with others by looking for similarities with the way of thinking, are they using me, what do they want from me, are they screwing with my mind to hurt me. I have been affected mentally by thinking of a way to get back at her somehow with the same results, spiritually prevents me from connecting with my God. emotionally feeling sadness, anger, and fear.

*He explains how his disease affected him by making him lazy, tired, and overweight, and not listening to other people and unable to connect to a higher power, causing him anxiety, fear and self-sabotage. He describes how his addiction manifested in internet dating, internet porn, and hiring escorts. He was obsessed with getting back at me.*

*This was very clear as he tormented me every single day from morning till night for 11 years after we divorced.*

*I myself suffered beyond words, anxious, scared, watching over my shoulder often felt my life and that of my children was threatened which in turn made me build a very strong shell and defense mechanism in order to survive and get through every day, especially protecting my babies.*

*He was out of control, and I carried this stress and weight alone.*

9. Yes I have given plausible but untrue reasons for my behavior which have been that I live alone, and that noone will tell me what to do or how to conduct myself when I violate myself, but in fact know that I am not honest with myself.

10. I had compulsively acted on the obsession of an escort that I used to date and got her involved in the real-estate of myself and sisters since she was also a real-estate agent, and would think that she would become my girlfriend without paying. That happened last year, 2010.

11. I had blamed my older sister and her husband that they didn't like her and that they didn't want to sell the property and that they were getting in between the ~~relation~~ false relationship of me and my girlfriend.

12. I had compared my addiction with others addiction as pot is used by doctors, lawyer, engineers and is a casual drug as opposed to alcohol, where I would label them as alcoholics, or heroin where I would label them as junkies.

## The Truth Revealed

*He became obsessed with an escort thinking she would become his girlfriend and not have to pay her anymore.*

*He blamed his family for not liking her and actually thought it was a real relationship he had but admits it was nothing but fake.*

*He thought his addictions were normal because pot is used by doctors and lawyers and other types of professionals.*

*He would call people who drank "alcoholics" and that junkies were people who used heroin, but that pot was just a casual drug.*

*Hi "casual" drug was nothing but destruction to my life and that of my children. He claims that he wasn't honest with himself by thinking that he should isolate himself by not having anyone tell him what to do.*

13) I was composing a current manifestation before I got clean or a least I'm not using drugs, and with time as honesty sets in with myself and my sponsor, but not plagued with the idea that I should no better as I'm understanding this disease.

14) Although, I have taken a University course in addictions, I still and continue to take information from other addicts to recover, and working on myself to be aware of my behavior and recognize before I act.

15) I did avoid acting on working this first step because I was afraid and ashamed for the things I have done in the past. At the convention I attended demonstrated to me and gave me the courage to share this first step with my sponsor. Some of the things I have done, other addicts have done the same.

16) The crisis that brought me to recovery was, that I was put in jail by my x-wife and

## The Truth Revealed

*Although he took a university course on addiction, he continued to listen to information from other addicts to try and work on himself and recover. He knew he needed to be aware of his behavior before he acted. He had a difficult time taking the first step and sharing it with his sponsor because he was afraid and ashamed of the things he had done, until he realized that other addicts had also done the same.*

(34)

daughter that pressed charges for harrassment.

17. The situation that led me to work step one is my former sponsor which often told me that we were going to work closely together, and when I approached him on occasions he would either walk away in the middle of the conversation, or not give me some kind of guidance on how to start working step one. I then looked towards Dave and admired his recovery and his sponsees.

18. I first recognized my addiction as a problem as soon as I got out of jail. I tried to corrected by going to rehab in hamilton. and by going to NA one day after rehab for recovery.

19. I'm powerless over drugs and alcohol.

20. I have use the internet, and dating sites, & have thought of ways to get back at my x-wife and daughter, as to hurt them financially

21. using internet games and dating sites so as to hopefully get rid of the loneliness feeling knowing that it won't be the solution.

## The Truth Revealed

*The crisis that made him seek rehab was when my daughter and I pressed charges against him for harassment, where he was arrested and put in jail. He states he first recognized his addiction when he got out of jail.*

*The reason he got out of jail is I decided NOT to pursue charges against him in hopes he would understand. He finally did and admitted himself into rehab.*

*He admits to being powerless over drugs and alcohol. He also admits to having thought of ways (which he did exercise) in order to harm me and my daughter and using the internet to get rid of the feelings of loneliness learning it was NOT the solution.*

22. My personality changes when I'm acting out is that I get frustrated, and get even more lonely and angry, I tell myself why me - don't I deserve a nice girlfriend in my life. I get lazy and feelings of giving up on life.

23. I used to manipulate other people to get money so I could maintain my addiction by lying on expense account.

24. I have tried to quit on many occasions on my own but when other friends presented me the opportunity I took it. The pain emotionally would always resurfaced until I had to use again to numb it. There times where I stop were good and seemed brighter until I used again and the darkness came back. Tried to quit by getting married, then having children.

25. Addiction caused me to hurt myself in an emotional, physical, and spiritual way. Others that I would simply push away as I would isolate myself.

married then having children

## The Truth Revealed

*He used to manipulate people in order to get money to support his addiction.*

*He tried to quit on his own but any time the opportunity presented itself, he used again.*

*He claims he tried to quit by getting married and having children. Addiction caused him to hurt himself, push people away, and isolate himself.*

(36)

UNMANAGEABILITY.

26. Trouble at work was I was complaining a lot when little stupid things would bother me, impatient. couldn't wait to get out and use. School I would just get by with a passing grade, and tell myself (what is the use)

27. I would get angry, I would avoid family get togethers by lying and making excuses that I didn't really have.

28. I would talk behind their backs sometimes and would ~~ride~~ take rides. I would sometimes leave early at gatherings to isolate and use. lie, make excuses. blame

30. Unmanageability means to me my time as to appropriately set for cleaning, eating, paying my bills, always leaving things to the last minute, and beyond late payments of bills. not making arrangements before hand.

31. I was arrested for harassment on my daughter, and x. wife.

## The Truth Revealed

*He recalls his laziness in life, and how he would lie and avoid family gatherings because he just wanted to go use drugs and isolate himself. He would manage life badly, wait until the last minute to do things, and pay bills late, never arranging things beforehand.*

*He talks again about how he was arrested for harassment toward me and our daughter.*

(37)

32. I could have been arrested on many occasions.
→ driving while impaired, often and frequently used my drug while driving, often puffed some smoke while police was near by in traffic. I have punctured tires to my x-wife, and broke her window with a hockey puck of her bedroom residence.

33. did not often consider the needs of others but my own in active addiction and has caused my divorce to my wife and loss communication with my children.

34. Since a little while ago I have accepted responsibility for my life and my actions today I'm able to carry out my daily responsibilities, cause of my Home management without getting overwhelmed. This has affected my life as I don't have much stress, I am more calm. ALTHOUGH SOMETIMES I PANIC WITH FEAR.

35. I used to but since attending N/A regularly 120M/107 DAYS, I am a more patient and understanding person. How is that affected my life is that I take the time to make a decision or gone to resolve. and usually just plan minutes at a time. but then again I get angry at myself for not doing enough, like work on getting a job.

# The Truth Revealed

He confesses to having driven his car impaired and that he could have been arrested. He even did drugs, puffing the smoke with police nearby. He admits to having been the one who punctured my car tires and broken my bedroom window with a hockey puck and stole the things in my car.

> I only just found out it was him because of his confession. He had stolen my skates, my daughter's skates yet making it difficult for me to work without my skates. I had to find a way to buy new skates for me and my daughter.

He confirms that his active addiction was the reason he got divorced from me and lost communication with the children.

He claims to have accepted responsibility for his life and his actions. He also indicates he has been in meetings for addiction for 120 months and 107 days and is more patient because of it.

36. Since I have entered the N/A fellowship I remind myself of four principles that I work on a daily basis - 1) Be perfect with my word 2) don't make any assumptions 3) don't take anything personally and 4) always do my best. although my stinking thinking comes as plenty as it use to. less frequent and doesn't hurt

37. I do not maintain a crisis mentality responding with panic. I look towards reaching a reasonable way to resolve a situation, panic only increases fear and is or ends up being a waste of time. As I used to with my x-wife thinking she is brainwashing my kids, and telling monstrous things about me. As I answered that question a few days past and fear comes back a at N/A meeting shared about it and it got better, today Nov. 2, is a much better day.

38. I don't think so, but I know that I need to constantly be aware of how my addiction can manifest itself, but in general I am in good health.

39. I would say I either freeze in real danger or overreact when I was using felt like no adrenaline kicking in my system.

## The Truth Revealed

*The drug and addictive behavior made him have a temper tantrum claiming he used to think I was brainwashing the children against him but realizes differently now that he understands the truth.*

39

40. Physically I have not harmed anyone, emotional as a result of my addiction, I have harmed my children and my x-wife by leaving them instead of bringing up my addiction and seeking counseling.

41. Sometimes I have temper tantrums and when I'm in my car and I get pissed off because other cars cut in the line at the last minute to exit while I wait in line. or when they tailgate me. but not in public, no well my hand goes up.

42. Yes I did take drugs to suppress feelings for my father's death, and when I was sexually abused by a neighbor across the steet when I was 7 years old. my divorce, my children, my brothers death. did not want to feel any of that pain, use also to not feel all of the nice girls that wanted to get close to me. and pushed them away cause I didn't want them to know about my addiction.

*He says that physically he never harmed anyone but that emotionally, as a result of his addiction, he has harmed me and the children by leaving us instead of bringing up his addiction and seeking counselling.*

*He took drugs to suppress his feelings for his father's death and divulged that he was sexually abused at the age of seven by a neighbor across the street, his choice of divorce, his children, and the death of his brother. He was also having difficulty meeting women afraid they would find out about his addiction.*

*He realized much too late that he had a loyal supportive wife and two beautiful healthy children.*

(HO)

43. I have accepted the full measure of my disease. and know that if I am in the wrong frame of mind I am powerless.

44. No, I know I cannot associate with people connected with my addiction. I cannot go to those places where I used. drugs and paraphernalia where thrown out the day before I left for rehab.

45. I think I got through most of the pain, but will have to be with someone supportive when my mom passes away hopefully that will be a long time. And hopefully have enough clean time to realize that not an option to do. Work This Program to my advantage, I know it will see me through the rest of my life.

46. No I will not be able to control my using with enough clean time, I must remain abstinent from all drugs and alcohol.

47. There are no more reservations for me. No more cards in the deck! I have use up all of my reservations.

## The Truth Revealed

*He says that he has accepted the full measure of his disease and that if he is in the wrong frame of mind, he will become powerless.*

*He is aware that he cannot be around the same people and environments that connect him to his disease and cannot go anywhere that he will see drugs and other paraphernalia all of which were thrown out the day before he went to rehab.*

*He says that he feels he has gotten through most of the pain but recognizes he will need to be with someone supportive when his mother dies.*

*He says he will need to remain abstinent from drugs and alcohol for the rest of his life.*

*He writes, "There are no more reservations for me. No more cards in the deck. I have used up all my reservations."*

48. First couple of weeks I was afraid of surrender thinking N/A was kind of a cult and a different kind of class of people that I did not belong. and by coming back to meeting I could see that I had a lot in common with them, and then accepted that I was powerless over my addiction and that my life was unmanageable.

49. What convinces me that I can't use anymore is that my death (spirit, mental, emotions, physical, will deteriorate, and become once again unmanageable.

50. I accept I will never regain control cause if I take one it will lead up to more than a thousand again, I must remain abstinent for the rest of my life. I may have another relapse but I know I don't have another recovery.

51. I have completely surrender to my addiction, to my higher power to my sponsor, to myself and to n/a; I believe you must surrender before working the 1st step.

52. My life to would be lead by my higher power, and really have no control

## The Truth Revealed

*He describes how he thought Narcotics Anonymous wasn't the same class of people he was brought up with and describes it as a cult. After going back to meetings, he realized that they were just like him. He accepted he was powerless over his addiction and that his life was unmanageable.*

*He knows that if he doesn't stay clean, his health will deteriorate, and his life will become unmanageable again.*

59. I am following my sponsor direction, he has been a great part of my recovery, I feel his love, he is part of my higher power and his wife.

60. I go to meetings everyday sometimes twice a day now since July 5th.

61. Yes I am giving recovery my best effort, by going to meetings, doing service, step work and keeping in touch with my sponsor.

62. I did believe I was this terrible monster, in fact I believed since I was born on April 20 is the same as Adolph Hitler. And 4-20 was the time everyday to do my drug of choice. sort of not to sure of what this means.

63. Yes I do have a sense of my relative importance within my circle of family and friends, yes in a sense that I care for them and that if they need anything or support I will make time for them. my mother cares and worries about me and I know I should make myself more available for her, my sisters there are not really communicating together or with myself, but this situation has been

His sponsor and sponsor's wife were a big part of his recovery giving him the support he needed. He talks about having been to meetings once and even twice a day.

He was trying to give his recovery a chance by attending daily meetings, doing service, staying in close touch with his sponsor and working the step program.

> His next words were the reason I titled this book 4/20 A Mothers Fight To Survive

62. "I did believe I was this terrible monster, in fact I believed, since I was born on April 20, is the same as Adolph Hitler, and 4:20 was the time every day to do my drug of choice. Sort of not too sure of what this means."

He talks about having a circle of friends and family around him. He states that his mother cares and worries about him and how he needs to make more time for her.

> People today have less and less respect, appreciation, and gratitude for their parents. It is so important to keep those ties very, very tight and give parents the support and care they need as they did when we were being raised by them. Try and make parents happy the last stretch of life just like we had their hand throughout our lives, because when they die it will be consolation to know you treated them with love and patience, NOT PUNISHMENT.

(45)

going on for a long time, don't think it can change, I have tried through our family company to have more meetings but without success. In society I have been disconnected for a long time, for example the job market, and because of my using my isolation progressed. But I am looking for a job now and by attending s/r meetings and sharing I do feel that I have a lot to offer and care very much about a certain amount of members and feel that they care for me as well.

64. I am practicing the principle of humility in connection with this first step - by accepting the things I did in the past and what happened to my sexual abuse as a child, the money I have stolen from my mother's purse, from having cheated on my wife, for abandoning my children; and probably feel humility when I share with my sponsor, and by revealing to him all of my defects of character.

## The Truth Revealed

*He explains how he was disconnected from society because he would isolate himself to use drugs. He says that he was ready to find a job. He was practicing the principle of humility in connection with the first step by accepting what he did in the past and what happened with his sexual abuse when he was 7 years old, by a neighbor, the money he stole from his mother, from having cheated on me, and having abandoned our children.*

*He shares and reveals all of the defects in his character to his sponsor.*

2. Did I believe I could control my using? What were some of my experiences with this, and how were my efforts unsuccessful? I tried controlling my using by only using on holidays, then it went on to the weekends only, then after work, then it progressed from morning till bed-time. I found that instead of decreasing it actually increased my using.

3. What things did I do that I can hardly believe I did when I look back at them?
Did I put myself in dangerous situations to get drugs? Yes in Florida I drove around in getto neighborhoods asking to buy drugs, I asked prostitutes if they knew where I could buy drugs. Did I behave in ways of which I'm now ashamed? What were those situations like? I had called an escort when my wife and daughter were in Atlanta for skating competition, my son was in the house sleeping so I thought. The girl showed up and my son asked who she was I lied and said she is just waiting for a taxi and to go back to bed - he might of seen or heard what was going on. I am still ashamed of that today. Embarrassing.

## The Truth Revealed

*He drove around in Ghettos (dangerous neighborhoods) in Miami asking prostitutes for drugs. He confesses to having called an escort to our home in Florida, while I was away in Atlanta with my daughter for a figure skating competition while my son was in the house.*

*My son woke up and asked who that woman was and he lied to him and sent him back to bed. He might have seen and heard what was going on. My son was five years old at the time.*
*He claims feeling shame for what he did.*

> When I read that part of the journal, the only thing I feel is anger and the desire to throw up.

4. Did I make insane decisions as a result of my addiction? Did I quit jobs, leave friendships and other relationships, or give up on achieving other goals for no reason other than that those things interfered with my using? Yes did give up jobs, left friendships, left my wife and my kids for my addiction.

5. Did I ever physically injure myself or someone else in my addiction? no, but my drug of choice physically injured me in my health, I was overweight, did no exercise, bad eating habits.

6. How have I overreacted or underreacted to things. I have overreacted with my older sister about the band in Ste. Adèle not being sold, and that her husband is full of shit on being a realestate developer. underreacted about the serious nature of maybe having a criminal record.

*He states having left us for his addiction. His drug of choice injured his health and made him overweight, when he developed bad eating habits and he didn't exercise.*

7. How has my life been out of balance?
My life has been out of balance spiritually, where I need to meditate ½ hr. every morning, and I haven't been doing that, need to go to the gym 3 times a week.

8. In what ways does my insanity tell me that things outside myself can make me whole or solve all my problems? Using drugs? Compulsive gambling, eating, or sex seeking? Something else. I did think that money or sex seeking could perhaps compensate for drugs but realized that it is a big waste of time, and the only way to make me whole is by continuing my meeting, keep doing my step work, and practice my meditation on a regular basis.

9. Is part of my insanity the belief that the symptoms of my addiction (using drugs or some other manifestation) is my only problem. Perhaps that was the only causing problem but the fact is that there are still problems and p most likely there will be others. such as my x-wife and not being able to see my children. But today I can sit back and think and rationalize for a solution.

## The Truth Revealed

*His insanity from drug use resulted in compulsive gambling, eating, or sex seeking. He thought all these addictions would help him stay away from drugs but realized it was ALL nothing but a waste of time. He says the only thing that he had to stick to were his daily NA meetings, meditation, and continuing the step program. He thought he could be at a point to be able to rationalize solutions concerning me and the children but that never happened. He still continues to find ways to stop having to pay child support.*

> He dragged me to court for 10 years to find a way to stop paying child support.

(5)

10. When we've acted on an obsession, even though we knew what the results would be, what were we feeling and thinking beforehand? What made us go ahead. Usually it was that of the rationalization that if I'm not using then therefore it must be ok. I'm not using drugs so I can do anything else, how conniving. but now there are moments so the key is to do something else like cleaning or throw away some garbage or go for a walk, take a shower until that moment passes.

11. Do I have any fears about coming to believe? What are they?
I did have fears about coming to believe, and believe a god, because I thought to relate religion to god and the religion I was brought up with was very deceiving. and use to curse at him, and dare him to take my life. I thought he took my father's life, my brother and nephew

12. Do I have any other barriers that make it difficult for me to believe? What are they?

## The Truth Revealed

*When he would think about drugs, he said the key to overcoming that feeling was to do something else, such as clean his apartment or go to the gym until that moment would pass. He feared believing in God and felt the religion he was brought up in was deceiving. He would curse at God and dare him to take his life. He thought that God took his father, brother, and nephew.*

Not really this week god has answered me on many occasions example got a job interview, past my interview very successfully, got another call from another employer, passed a telephone interview, and was asked for a second interview, another call from my 1st interview for a finall interview with Marriot hotel manager. This god or higher power comes from many sources of confidence, such as my spouse that told me it would come.

13. What does the phrase "We came to beleive" mean to me? Well, I prayed to my higher power as my my financial worries were getting stronger, so I prayed for some kind of job (whichever) then I came to beleive that this higher power has answered me pretty convincingly as he gave me this job which is exactly what I wanted, but this took some time and some action.

14. Have I ever beleived in anything for which I didn't have tangible evidence? What was that experience like? I beleived that there was other life forms besides what we have on earth, that we weren't the only ones in the universe, and that man would eventually go to Mars and discover where life started,

*He believed that a God, or a higher power, helped him get a job interview and helped him secure the job he wanted. This is why he was encouraged to "come to believe" that the higher power was the reason for the job. He believed there were other life forms in the universe and that we would eventually find them on Mars.*

life, work, family, (meetings, meaning with myself.
28. How is restoration a process? Restoration is a process after 37 years of using, and first change your body, then your mind becomes clearer, over time, restoration comes over time.
29. How will working the rest of the steps help me in my restoration to sanity? They will help me discover more about myself and help me continue my recovery, and work on my defects of character over time.
30. How has sanity already been restored to me in my recovery? By discovering my higher power, and turning my life and my will over to him, and guiding me in my recovery along with my sponsor, the fellowship which has helped me grow
31. What expectations do I have about being restored to sanity? I expected to be restored to sanity just by stopping using drugs and stay clean, but realized that by working the steps, and living them, I and discovered that there is or are things greater then myself. I started to believe, and helped me restore my sanity.

## The Truth Revealed

*He learns that there is a "restoration process" which means that not using drugs allows your mind to become clearer and that this process happens over time. He felt the reason restoration happened was because he turned himself over to his higher power, his sponsor, and the fellowship of Narcotics Anonymous. He said that it will help him in his recovery and understanding himself and the defects of his character. He also believed that working the steps of the program is what will help him restore his sanity and not by just stopping the use of drugs.*

32. Are my realistic expectations about my recovery is progressing being met or not? Do I understand that recovery happens over time, not overnight? I do understand that it will take some time but also have to be more willing to do the work to progress in my step work and recovery.

33. Finding ourselves able to act sanely, even once, in a situation with which we were never able to deal successfully before is evidence of sanity. Have I had any experiences like that in my recovery? What were they? Just this morning, my uncle passed away, and when someone died in my family before, I used to use drugs more heavily to bury the emotional pain, this time around is feeling and remembering my uncle with all the good memories and how he lived a good life, and the dental work he done on me when I was a little kid, and how much I loved him.

## The Truth Revealed

*He said the recovery happens over time and not overnight. He used to use drugs even more when there was a death around him to overcome the pain but after rehab, he tried to focus on remembering the good memories.*

(63)

③ What action have I taken to follow through on my decision? I set myself realistic goals and follow through with them daily, I continue to go to meetings, and keep in touch with my sponsor, and continue to do my step work. And continue to believe and have faith.

④ What areas of my life are difficult for me to turn over? My broken marriage and the fact I can't see my now adult children growing.

⑤ Why is it important that I turn them over anyway? Because I will be angry everyday and my life will turn negative and will end up relapsing.

⑥ How have I acted on self-will? What were my motives? I have acted on self-will by leaving my wife and my kids, thinking I would have peace and quiet in my head, and my motives were <u>drugs</u> and <u>sex</u> with other women.

⑦ How has acting on self-will affected my life? Self will has left a very destructive path.

*He talks about the difficulty of turning over parts of his life and uses the example of his broken marriage and not seeing the children because of what he did. He explains how self-will made him leave me and the children and his motives were drugs and sex with other women and how self-will has left a very destructive path.*

behind me, and it seems that I can't have a second chance to fix it or at least apologize for what I have done to my wife and my children, and even though I pray to have my higher power relieve the pain, it's not enough.

⑧ How has my self-will affected others?
My SW is probably affecting my mother the most because I don't call her enough and I know she cares and loves me very much, but I don't want to discuss how I'm hurting inside because it would make her feel sad.

⑨ Will pursuing my goals harm anyone? How?
Pursuing my goals will not hurt anyone, because my goal is to do the best I can at my job, stay clean and work my program, my goal is to be back in my kids lives but still remains a struggle to think that it's been all my fault and my kids do not want me back in their lives.

⑩ In pursuing what I want, is it likely that I will end up doing something that adversely affects myself or others? explain. I'm only hurting myself but I can only go through the never ending pain, until somehow I will get an answer, I am only praying in the meantime.

## The Truth Revealed

*He prayed to his higher power because he felt he hadn't had the chance to fix or apologize to us all for what he had done. He felt his mother was affected the most because he knew she loved him and knows that the situation must have caused her deep harm. He understood that harming a mother was detrimental in life. He wrote that one struggle for him was to think how he hoped to be back in the children's lives and admits how it was all his fault for what had happened and that he felt the children didn't want him in their lives.*

(65)

11. Will I have to compromise any of my principles to achieve this goal? I hope and pray that I don't compromise my fellowship or my recovery work. But I will remain honest, loyal, and good to myself and others.

12. Describe the times when my will hasn't been enough? Didn't even have to read the example I knew right away that I true quitting drugs on self will or will-power as I used to call it, both simply or difficultly could not do it.

13. What is the difference between my will and god's will? My will is to get up in the morning and try my best, god's will will do the rest, and therefore the outcome at the end of the day is positive. Instead of my will or self will or will power is a lot less effective.

14. Have there been times in my recovery when I've found myself subtlly taking back my will and my life? What alerted me? What have I done to recommit myself to the third step?

15. A few times this has happened while working with an x-colleague, I was getting

*He explained how he tried to stop using drugs with his own self-will but understood that he couldn't do it without help.*

frustrated, and angry cause I was doing half her work and all of mine. What alerted me was to go back to the basics, to do my best and god will take care of the rest eventually! I would soon recommit by looking up, and say to myself that I have no control and that he (God) is driving my life.

15. Does the word God or even the concept itself, make me uncomfortable? What is the source of my discomfort? I used to just shiver with discomfort cause I it me back to the religion I was brought into, the catholique God which is not the God I understood, the father of Jesus.

16. Have I ever believed that God caused horrible things to happen to me or was punishing me? What were those things? I believed that God took my dad away, and my brother, and my kids away after my divorce, and begged him to take my life either by lightning or some natural disaster.

17. What is my understanding of a Power greater than myself today? This Power can be different every day, it can be the Sun, the wind, the clouds, the sky, it can be planes, control

*He believed that God took his father, brother, and the kids away from him and begged him to take his life either by lightning or some natural disaster.*

30. Have there been times when I have been to do to let go and trust god for the outcome? yes in me getting a job, and letting go of my children and x-wife, and my financial worries, how will I make ends meet.

31. How do I take action to turn it over? Are there any words I say regularly? what are they? yes ("thank-you.) I will try my best.)

32. What am I doing to reinforce my decision to allow my higher power to care for my will and my life? I try to keep an open mind especially at work and let the day unroll itself instead of trying to control it. on my days off I rest and sometimes I'm hard on myself by telling myself to get off my ass but I really do need my rest.

33. How does the third step allow me to build on the surrender I've developed in steps one and two? it allows me to reflect on where I was in step one and two, it's like a reflection on where I was and where I am now, less nervous or fearful, I guess its the surrender, and letting my god of understanding take my will and my life.

*He believed that he needed to turn over his worries to God, such as the children, me, and his worries of how to make ends meet. His way of turning his worries over was to say thank you every day and that he would try his best in life. He practiced allowing life to take its course and, on his days off, to allow himself to rest.*

34. In what ways have I demonstrated willingness in my recovery so far? My willingness really began after step one, when I took action to send my C.V. out for a job and really progressed through my job, and really practice that throughout my work days.

35. Am I fighting anything in my recovery? What do I think would happen if I became willing to let recovery prevail in that area of my life? I don't really know if I could call that fighting or wanting something, my x-wife and kids back into my life, perhaps its more like hoping for that to happen and then telling myself that its not going to happen at the same time don't really know if I am better off without them although lots of changes has happened on both sides.

36. How have hope, faith, and trust become positive forces in my life? I can feel and see that in myself more so at work, as I am confident on my abilities, to listen before I answer, take proper action to direct our guests at the hotel without getting impatient or intollerable, and willing

*He writes, "Am I fighting anything in my recovery? Don't really know if I would call that fighting or wanting something, my ex-wife and my children back in my life, perhaps it's more like hoping for that to happen and then telling myself that it's not going to happen at the same time don't really know if I am better off without them although lots of changes have happened on both sides."*

and anxious to get up the next day to do it again.

37. What further action can I take to apply the principles of hope, faith, and trust in my recovery? I can further take action by trusting myself more by also connecting with my higher power that no matter what happens with my x-wife and kids, everything will work out the way they are suppose to.

38. What evidence do I have that I can trust confidently in my recovery? Although at work, things can be very hectic, and out of control, I'm still patient and confident that at the end of the day all will be well, and that the thought of using because of these work days which are sometimes insane don't even enter my mind is phenomenal!

STEP 4. We made a searching and fearless moral inventory of ourselves.

1. Do I have any reservations about working this step? What are they? Not sure but maybe my x-wife and kids.

2. What are some of the benefits that could come from making a searching and fearless moral inventory of myself? Most likely to go to the root of what started my addiction with drugs and face my fears.

## The Truth Revealed

*He deduced that he was to let go and let his higher power decide his fate and believe that whatever happens, it will be what is meant to be. He had reservations about working step 4 because he would have to face dealing with me and the children and what he did to us. He needed to get to the root of what started his addiction and face it.*

I'm still dealing with financial consequences from my mom's death. Government I resent, and corrections such as lawyers and judges who make decisions for us instead of my higher power.

13. What was my motivation, or what did I believe, that led me to act as I did in these situations. I thought maybe by getting married would stop my using or perhaps cut down.

14. How has my dishonesty contributed to my resentments? dishonesty with myself and others, have led me to making the wrong decisions with my marriage and divorce and everything else in my life. Therefore now regreting what I have done and said.

15. How has my inability or unwillingness to experience certain feelings led me to develop resentments? fear of facing situations with honesty, and keeping it to myself, has led me with these resentments. Instead of discussing these situations as soon as they arise.

16. How has my behavior contributed to my resentments? - well instead of running away I face these situations - which don't create unnecessary fear or anger.

## The Truth Revealed

*He thought that getting married and having kids would make him stop doing drugs. Instead of running away he learned to face his problems so not to have unnecessary fear or anger. He regrets all that he did and said.*

*The recuperation and chance for a normal life is something that must happen now for me and my children.*

# THE AIR I BREATHE

WHILE I WAS dealing with this monster of an estate, this posed a stressful period for the whole family. I provided everything I could for my children and sacrificed myself only to give them safety and love the best way I knew how.

This is something no one can take away from me.

My children are my life and the reason I exist. I just pray that one day they will realize who I am and what I did and honor me, protect me, and love me unconditionally. I long to have them call me for no reason, include me in their lives, and make me feel like a priority. I hope that they will understand how much I need them more than ever know. I just want to feel loved by them. They are the air I breathe. I don't want to suffer anymore but they don't seem to understand and just want it all to go away. HE is GONE! We can finally have a healthy and close family, but I can't do it alone. So, I wait and hope I can have that chance to feel love and happiness with them.

My best friend, who has loved me unconditionally and stood by me since 2009 through thick and thin finished reading this book on Feb 24, 2024 and immediately sent me a message saying, *"I just finished reading your book and my sincere wish for you is that your children read it and understand so that your future with them erases everything from the past, so that you can become the person you would have been had you not suffered such deep and difficult traumas."* He damaged me and created a life of difficulty that became the norm and were my daily patterns. I didn't know how to change them. Now, there is only one thing that will fix and erase my past.

    I need it in order to break the 30-year cycle and have a chance to spend what's left of my life in peace. I need love and to be held in my children's arms with their support and understanding. I continue to pray for this.

# A Mother's Message

I END THIS book with a very important and strong message to my children and to every family that suffers severe trauma.

Always stay close to your roots. Your roots are your lifeline and life cannot be healthy without the blessings of a mother, her sacrifices, and family.

There are many ways to deal with past trauma. You can attack it head on with an open mind, being aware and seeing the work, dealing with its pain, and helping others by creating awareness. Or you can ignore it, try to pretend it's not there and continue in the same pain which I promise you will stay with you and pass on to the next generation. Having patience and understanding is something we must always have with our roots, never walking away from those who suffered for us. Honoring and learning from examples is something important. Never hold grudges as they are a poison to a family. Allowing the past to continue to hurt you is a personal choice that only you can be accountable for. For me, dealing with it is and will always be the only way to become free.

I want both my children to know that I'm grateful for their existence and their courage. Apart from the normal family conflicts that exist in any family, I am proud of them and love them even when they made bad choices. Today they have built their lives the way they wanted and all I wish for them is health, comfort, and gratitude. They too suffered and they should know that I recognize this and always did. I pray for a family unit that is united with love and respect from them both for the rest of our lives and that we can spend healthy moments together.

As Maya Angelou wrote in "Still I Rise". It is now time to Rise!

Love,
Mama

# Resources

## First Steps

Call the police

Go to your local hospital

Reach out to your place of worship

Google shelters for women in your area

Reach out to family, friends, and neighbors

## Additional Resources

**NWSN** (National Women's Shelter Network)
https://nationalwomensshelternetwork.org/

**Women Against Violence Europe** (46 countries)
https://wave-network.org/

**Assaulted Women's Helpline** (Canada)
https://www.awhl.org/

# BE THE FIRST TO KNOW

Follow Alice Nehme on Instagram to learn about upcoming book signings, readings, and new releases.

https://linkpro.cz/Ah2pgNr

www.ingramcontent.com/pod-product-compliance
Lightning Source LLC
LaVergne TN
LVHW020109100426
835512LV00041B/3315